Shaped to Fit

How God changes a young woman to prepare her for an unexpected destiny.

Joan Kearney

Onwards and Upwards Publishers

3 Radfords Turf
Cranbrook
Exeter
EX5 7DX
United Kingdom

www.onwardsandupwards.org

This first edition published in the United Kingdom by Onwards and Upwards Publishers (2017).

ISBN: 978-1-911086-69-7
Typeface: Sabon LT
Editor: Victoria Lyle
Graphic design: LM Graphic Design

Printed in the United Kingdom.

Endorsements

While Joan's heroic victory over a tarantula left me shaking all over, Andy's story brought tears to my eyes. This book's worth it for those two passages alone, but her honest accounts of a slightly bizarre upbringing and then ten years living in the jungle exchanged later for rural England and a spell in the Himalayas leave me amazed at the depth of what God has done in Joan's life.

Dr Val Inchley OBE
Has served in medical work in Nepal for forty-three years.

We live in a world where we have learned to fear extremism to such an extent that we cannot differentiate between evil and good. A superficial reading of this book may lead one to believe that even if the extremism is good it is still pointless. Who would wish to worship and follow someone who allowed such pain and loss? Yet Joan takes us carefully and gently by the hand to reveal a love that is incomprehensible to the selfish and self-centred heart but gloriously wonderful to the soul that can recognise its own inadequacies. Oh, for a few more Joans in this needy lost world!

Danny M. Batten BSc FCPFA DMS
Former Director of Finance for Devon and Cornwall Magistrates' Courts.
Now president of CIPFA Southwest Regional Council.

This book is an interesting yet simple read by an unassuming woman whose life has been full and varied – from learning and writing down the language of a remote Brazilian tribe and working in the mountain area of Nepal to fulfilling the duties of a minister's wife in rural England. Joan has been honest and vulnerable about the pressures and battles that we so often go through in our lives.

This is a book that can be picked up and put down without losing the thread of a story that demonstrates the many and varied ways that God seeks to fulfil his goal of transformation of our character.

Rev. Peter Milner BA (Hons)
Minister of Queensberry Baptist Church, Nottingham.

About the Author

Joan's childhood in a strict Christian sect formed her into an ill-at-ease, shy, prim-and-proper young woman. Her book describes the adventures and surprises, the struggles and failures, the sadness and the joy that have been transforming her into a very different person. Now in retirement, she looks back over the eighty exciting years so far and shares something of what she has been discovering about life. And about God.

Author's Note

My story includes references to a number of people whose lives have touched, helped and inspired mine, particularly my family, friends and colleagues. But there are hundreds more whose names are not mentioned here. Thank you all. I have needed you and been grateful for you.

I've led a very varied life, so much so that I often think I've become a Jack-of-all-trades-and-master-of-none! But it has been a wonderfully interesting and varied experience and when, from time to time, I've mentioned my adventures to someone, they've often commented, "You should write your life story." For a long time I've resisted, not wanting to be at the centre of attention. There came a day, however, when I began to realise that I am not at the centre of my own story; rather, God is the producer and stage director of the 'play' – hopefully not like Shakespeare's description of life as "a poor player who struts and frets their hour upon the stage and then is heard no more"!

I recently read a wonderful autobiographical book by Margaret Spufford[1] in which she says:

> *I am indeed amazed that out of the vast confusion of my own reality anything of value seems to have emerged, but, if it has, it does not feel as if I were responsible, rather as if, despite the poor quality of the canvas, the Artist has managed to say something after all.*

She expresses beautifully how I feel. May the great Artist say something through all our lives!

Joan Kearney

---

[1] © Margaret Spufford, 1996, *Celebration, A Joy of Suffering,* Continuum UK, used by permission of Bloomsbury Publishing Plc.

Contents

Prologue

Who is This Woman?

It was a hot afternoon. The villagers were quiet, resting until the day cooled. The English woman was in her hammock too, reading. Soon the children would be coming around, ready to go swimming with her in the river. Or someone would be coming for malaria medicine. Or asking if she had any spare fish-hooks. Just now she was enjoying a time of peace.

Until a shout at her door meant she had visitors – Portuguese-speaking visitors. This was an occasion. She got to her feet, ran a hand through her hair and called a welcome,

"Vamos chegar! Boa tarde." ("Come in. Good afternoon.")

The door opened and two unknown men came in. They quickly explained that they were from a gold-prospecting camp about an hour away by canoe.

"Our gaffer needs medical help. We all had a lot of drink yesterday. The supply-boat had been by and we had a crate of pinga." (cheap Brazilian spirit) "Our gaffer fell near the fire and he's burnt his hand. And it brought on malaria today. He needs an injection. We've to take you down to the camp today with your syringe and some Aralen."

There was a slight unease in her mind, a note of caution. "No, you go back and tell him I'll be along soon. I'll get two of the tribesmen to bring me down, so that I've got transport to bring me back again. See you soon!" And off they went.

For her an outing like this was a pleasant change. The two tribesmen looking after her were officially her nephews in the tribal system that had adopted her, but they usually called her "mother" and were supportive and helpful. Away from the house, being paddled downriver by these two young fellows, she felt on holiday, trailing a hand in the cool water and delighting in the jungle scenery.

But arriving at the prospectors' camp, she was business-like again as she prepared the medication. She was feeling that the man's troubles were his own fault so she continued being helpful but was not too friendly or compassionate. The two tribesmen who had brought her from the village kept their distance but watched warily. The English woman completed her task, suggested that the patient should come up to the village if any further treatment was needed and said her goodbyes.

As her two 'sons' paddled the boat upstream again, Joan Kearney was thinking. The patient was not nearly as ill as she had been led to believe. Why on earth had they taken the trouble to come and get her? On reflection, she began to think that it might have been for very different motives. Motives linked with the isolation of their camp, the pinga they had been drinking, and her being one of the very few single Portuguese-speaking women in the area, an area hundreds of miles away from police availability.

How does a young British girl from Bolton with a traditional upbringing end up living with a remote tribe far from comfort and safety? In this book, Joan tells her story and shows how we are each like pieces in a divine jigsaw puzzle – our purpose becomes clear when God connects us with others and fits us into the beautiful picture he is creating.

Chapter One

Early Childhood

1936 - 1941

Bryan was clever. He was a boy, the eldest and, it seemed to me, quietly confident of his ability to do anything better than his two sisters! He was fifteen months older than Hilary, and still not three years old when I was born.

Hilary was charming. When visitors came to the house, she would sit on their lap and chat to them while Bryan and I hid under the table. It was covered with a big, brown chenille cloth and a good place for hiding. I didn't think Bryan was nervous. I felt as if he was there because he didn't want his life to be interrupted by having to be nice to people. Or maybe he was just keeping his little sister company! I was there because I was frightened of them. They asked questions and wanted me to reply, and I blushed and felt silly and wished they would go away.

There were lots of visitors. Our parents belonged to a strange group of Christians known as the Exclusive Brethren, where men were referred to as "brothers" and women as "sisters". The Brethren were narrow in their thinking, and felt superior to anyone who wasn't "one of us", but they were very hospitable and caring towards others in the same group. Hence all those visitors. On Sunday dinner times, when we came home from the Meeting, the best crockery came out of the sideboard, Mummy was in vivacious visitor-mode, and I quietly endured and hoped I wouldn't have to get involved in the conversation. Daddy was quieter than Mummy, but would do his best to be the gracious host, and was very alive and interested whenever people talked about the Bible or questions of theology. The sisters all kept quiet then – theological discussion was for the brothers.

I think my mother must have spoiled me. Her father had died just before I was born and it's possible that she found comfort in her new baby. I remember her telling people that I was "a good little thing". That contrasted with Bryan and Hilary, who were braver souls, much more adventurous than I. Mummy used to tell us about a morning when she'd been upstairs changing my nappy and came down to find Bryan and Hilary sprinkling talcum powder liberally on the cushions of the settee and enjoying the clouds of "smoke" as they beat them with wooden spoons.

When I was three, Mummy had to go into hospital for an operation. The days that she was away felt like a desert to me. A sister called Miss Butterfant came to stay and look after us. I spent a lot of the time in tears, and Miss Butterfant said I was a spoilt little girl and needed to pull myself together. Bryan, Hilary and I sat on the stairs to complain to one another about her. We secretly called her "Miss Butter Pants" and felt we were getting our own back and being very unkind. I enjoyed that. Not such a good little thing after all.

I remember another occasion after Mummy was back home again, when Bryan, now five or six years old, took me to sit on those same stairs and hear a very naughty poem that he'd learned from a boy at school. It had bad words in it, so I had to promise not to tell the grown-ups. The poem was:

Bah humbug! Botheration!
Three cats in one station.

That was all!

It wasn't only Miss Butterfant who thought I was a spoilt little girl. About that time I had to go to the dentist to have a tooth out. In those days, the dentist's surgery was the front room of his house so when I was too afraid to open my mouth and was struggling to get out of the chair, the dentist called in his wife to hold me down. I'm sorry to say that I bit her hand, and she pronounced me the naughtiest little girl she had ever met. In the end, I remember hearing that they had given me gas and, once I was unconscious, he had been able to extract the offending tooth.

But there were some times when I was truly naughty. One was on Hilary's birthday. She had been given a chocolate smoker's set – pipes and cigarettes made of delicious milk chocolate. That wouldn't be politically correct nowadays, and even then, nobody in our family smoked. But made of chocolate – that was something else! That chocolate was on my mind all of teatime. I ate quickly and asked to get down from the table before the others. I went to find Hilary's present, and stole a chocolate cigarette. When everyone else left the table, Hilary quickly discovered that one of the cigarettes was missing. I asserted that I knew nothing about it, but was belied by the melted chocolate on my hands and around my mouth.

Chocolate binges would soon be a thing of the past, however. That was the year when the Second World War began, and soon sweets of all kinds would be severely rationed.

I was three. The outbreak of war stayed in my mind even though the words meant nothing to me at that time. Daddy had taken us all to Fleetwood on holiday, and had taken rooms in someone's house. That was a great system. The landlady did the cooking and the cleaning; the guests did their own meal planning and shopping – that way, my parents could afford a three-week holiday instead of the usual fortnight. That landlady had a problem with our surname, Boswood – she thought it was "Rosewood". One day, as we were eating our tea, she was listening to the radio and came into the dining room in great distress. "Oh, Mr and Mrs Rosewood," she said, "we're at war!" I've no memory of what anyone else said or what happened next, but I was aware of the anxiety in the room and my puzzlement about what was making the grown-ups unhappy.

So far as I was concerned, life carried on as normal. We lived in Bolton, so we were not likely to suffer much from the Blitz. Daddy's job in the Civil Service exempted him from being called up to serve in the armed forces. Mummy was well again. Our "daily" went to work in a munitions factory where she could earn a lot more than working as a domestic helper. Hilary started going to school. We were all issued with gasmasks in case of chemical warfare. True to form, I made a fuss when mine was tried on, because I didn't like the smell of the rubber. What a wimp! My life was Mondays to Fridays at home with Mummy, Saturdays to the park or the sweet shop where we each had a penny to spend, and Sundays to the Meeting with the whole family.

We had special Sunday Meeting clothes, even when clothing coupons limited the amount of clothes we could buy. Bryan would have a clean shirt and short trousers, worn with his school tie, blazer and cap. Daddy wore a suit and tie, of course, and his homburg hat, and carried a rolled umbrella. Mummy wore silky dresses, and a matching coat and hat. Underneath would be various large and firmly boned items. It's astonishing how underclothes have become smaller and smaller and so much less restrictive in the few decades of our lives. Hilary and I would wear a vest and Liberty bodice, except in the height of summer. That's astonishing too – now that most of us have centrally heated houses, we all wear fewer layers of clothing than was normal in my childhood. Over that we would have, in summer, a dress and cardigan; in winter, a kilt and jumper. And, inevitably, a matching coat, hat and gloves. Being the younger sister, my clothes were nearly all hand-me-downs. One of my aunties knitted me a striped jumper in blue wool and fluffy white angora. I absolutely adored it, but hardly ever wore it because I didn't have a skirt to match. One of the tragic moments of my young life was finding that I'd become too big for that treasured jumper made especially for me.

At the Meeting we sat on rows of chairs around a central table. The Meeting room was unadorned. There was a row of pegs where the men and boys could put their hats. Women and girls had to keep their hats on, because the Bible says that women must have their heads covered when they pray. We also all had long hair – the girls with bunches or plaits tied with neatly ironed ribbons, the women with their hair in a roll or a bun secured with hairpins. There was no vicar or priest at our Meetings. All the brothers could pray, if they wished, or suggest a hymn, which would be sung unaccompanied. Between the hymns and prayers, we sat in silent contemplation. I don't remember what I contemplated when I was very young, but I remember working out hockey manoeuvres and having a surreptitious chat with my sister using deaf-and-dumb sign language as a teenager. The morning service was always a Communion, which we called "the breaking of bread". The table would be covered with a crisply starched, white cloth, and laid with a loaf of bread and a chalice of wine. The motivation for such simplicity was to avoid any emphasis on what is external, in order that everyone could focus on what is internal – their own relationship with God. There was no Sunday school for children, and I didn't actually enjoy those quiet Sunday mornings. If that was something God liked, I thought He must be quite a boring person, very tight-lipped and disapproving.

Soon I was five and joined my brother and sister at a little private school in the centre of Bolton. At playtime, we were ushered into a small, paved playground with what seemed like hordes of small boys charging around. You can imagine how this shy, quiet, spoilt little girl felt. One of the big boys (he must have been all of nine years old) put his tongue out at me as he raced by. I dissolved into tears and had to be taken inside to play with the dolls' house.

After a few weeks there, I was getting bolder and quite enjoying some of my schoolwork. One part I didn't enjoy, however, was when our teacher was filling in the register at the beginning of afternoon school. To keep us occupied, she gave us the task of copying out the two-times table, not just once, but every day, or so it seemed to me. On the third day, my boredom could take no more. I went out to the teacher, already busy with the register, and said the job was too hard for me. "I can't do it, Miss." My punishment was to spend the rest of the afternoon in the babies' class, with those who weren't yet five. She thought I'd feel humiliated, but actually I quite enjoyed it – except for trying to explain to my mother why I was in the wrong class when she arrived to take us home!

After I'd had a couple of terms at that school, we moved to a neighbouring town, Bury, because my dad's job was now in the Bury office. There we lived in an old-fashioned house on the A56, two miles north of the town, and Hilary and I went to the local primary school. My parents must have been retrenching at that stage, because there was no domestic help for Mum, and only Bryan went to a fee-paying school in town.

My first day at the new school didn't quite meet my expectations. Not because we didn't wear a uniform there, nor because my new classmates spoke with a more marked Lancashire accent than those at the "nice" school in Bolton. No, those things didn't bother me. In fact, I soon developed a good accent myself: King's English at home; Lancashire at school. What upset me that first day was Miss

Moorhouse. I was quite a bright child and could already read fairly fluently. Miss Moorhouse asked me to stay in at playtime and tried me out with a book about a farm. Was the farmer called Old Lob? If you're of my generation, you may remember him. I read the book without difficulty. To my astonishment, the teacher didn't say anything complimentary, just sent me out to play without a word. With hindsight I can guess now that she was thinking, "What a conceited little girl! She's obviously not going to fit in my class. I'll pass her on to Mrs Gill." So to Mrs Gill's class I went, feeling bewildered and unappreciated.

Behind my "good little thing" exterior was quite a sad person. Perhaps being the youngest in the family is part of the reason. Whatever I learned to do was old hat because Bryan and Hilary could do it so much better. As the years went on, when Bryan began to learn Latin, we were all impressed and willingly gave time to test him on his "amo, amas, amat". By the time I started Latin lessons, nobody thought anything of it. When Hilary was in the First XI hockey team, we found that exciting. When I made the First XI a year later, I don't remember bothering to tell them at home.

Writing down these memories, I don't like this child very much. I may have looked sweet, but I was self-centred, spineless and jealous. That's not the person I'd want to have been.

At Morecambe – upset because Mum wasn't there!

Chapter Two

Family Relationships

1942 - 1954

Dad loved nature, and we learned to love it too. House martins nested each year under the eaves of our house: heart-breaking when a baby bird fell to its death on the path below; awe-inspiring when the fledglings learned to fly.

One spring day, as the family were having our tea, Dad said he was going to take us for a walk to show us something exciting. He wouldn't tell us what it was, so it was with anticipation that we later walked up the main road, past the church and our school, beyond the place where the houses finished and the fields began, across the fields and into a little wood with a stream running through it. Dad asked us to sit very still on one bank of the stream and not to talk; just to look at the other bank. And as we watched, a robin came down with food in its mouth and disappeared into the undergrowth. There was a chirruping, and then it reappeared without the food and flew away. We sat entranced for some time as the parent birds fed their nestlings, and then we crept away home. It was a magical evening.

Another time we were out with Dad on a winter's day, walking on frozen snow as deep as the Pennine walls were high. That day we saw a hare running up the hillside, its brown fur standing out against the whiteness of the snow.

It was amazing that Dad could be such a good father to us. He had grown up in London, and his own father had died of tuberculosis when

Dad was only seven. His mother had been left a widow with four children and a fifth on the way. The baby later died, also of TB. With incredible courage, Grandma had brought up her son and three daughters in considerable poverty. We have a photo of Dad's class at school, when he was about ten years old. All the other boys are dressed in little jackets with stiff shirt collars and bow ties. Dad – the scholarship child – is the only one in a knitted woollen jumper.

He had to leave school at sixteen and go to work in a bank to supplement the family income. But travelling to work on the Tube, he would be studying – reading encyclopaedias to build up his general knowledge. At twenty-one he sat a Civil Service exam where the other applicants were university graduates. They didn't all pass, but he was one of those who did, and he became an Inspector of Taxes. It wasn't that he enjoyed the humdrum office work he had to do. He did it because it was a safe job that would bring in enough money to look after a house and family.

His mother was not only courageous. She was also a woman of deep piety. I knew her as an old lady, very deaf (her hearing-aid was a heavy black box of batteries on her lap with headphones on her head), and very crippled with arthritis (no-one had yet heard of replacement hips and knees). She must have lived with constant frustration and pain, but the tag line we all remember her saying again and again was, "My dears, we have so much to be thankful for." When she died, she was sitting up in bed reading her Bible, where her daughters heard her singing a children's hymn:

Jesus loves me, this I know
For the Bible tells me so.

Minutes later, they took a tray of breakfast in to her, but she had just gone to heaven to meet the One she'd been singing about.

When my dad died, he left a list of the hymns he wanted us to sing at his funeral. The first was one he remembered his mother singing. When she put her four young children to bed, she would sit at the top of the stairs, singing to settle them to sleep. One of their favourites was:

Safe in the arms of Jesus,
Safe on his gentle breast,

There by his love o'ershaded
Sweetly my soul shall rest.

They are words with an old-fashioned ring to our twenty-first century ears, but full of peace and comfort to a lonely widow and her fatherless children.

His background had made my dad someone to admire – a man of faith, whose effort and perseverance had overcome considerable obstacles. But he had been the only male in an otherwise all-female household. His way of coping was to speak derisively of female foibles and failings. My sister and I both remember him calling us a "silly goose" when we couldn't understand our maths homework. Bryan's education was important to him. But he thought I should leave school at sixteen and get a job, because further education would be wasted on a woman.

Dad found it very difficult that, with a reasonably good brain and many advantages, I had a problem working consistently and perseveringly. I loved reading, day-dreaming, and being free. I struggled with things that had to be done – keeping rules, being in a straitjacket. That meant that Dad was sometimes very critical of me. He may have been trying to balance Mum's over-indulgence of her youngest, but to me it felt like, "Dad doesn't like me." There was a phase in my early teens when I cried myself to sleep, thinking about him and wishing I could do something to make him like me. It was also partly because of the difference between Hilary and me. Dad was a reserved, shy man, but when we were small, Hilary would climb onto his lap and when we were older, she'd sometimes tease him or be a little bit cheeky to make him smile. Those were things I couldn't do. I was similar to him, shy too, and I could only hang back.

The other male in our family was my brother, nearly three years older than I was. Once, when I'd started going to the High School in town, I was sitting on the tram at the terminus on my way home, when I saw Bryan coming for the same tram. I was so pleased, hearing him get on and come upstairs to where I was. But he walked past without a glance. I didn't know then that big boys are often embarrassed by their younger sisters. I just felt my heart sink to my boots with rejection and unworthiness. Mum and Hilary were usually nice to me. But I thought that they must just be kind for the sake of it. The men in my family, it seemed, didn't like me.

Once, in my teens, I said something that Dad found very painful. We were talking about whether I'd be able to carry on studying and be a teacher, which was my dream at the time. Dad was saying it was a waste of money. I blurted out, "Look, Dad, if I'm too expensive, I'm sorry. But I didn't ask to be born." He referred to it several times in later years, incredibly hurt. I was sad I'd upset him, but never quite understood why.

Dad thought that too much education was a waste of money because girls got married and became housewives. But in the event, that argument was flawed in my case, because this girl didn't get married for a very long time.

During my school years, I had crushes on various lads, but if there was ever a possibility of being someone's girlfriend, I'd back off, knowing that I was not really loveable, thinking I must have imagined that this one or that one liked me. Once, in junior school, some of the other children held me, fighting to get free, while a boy called Fred Pilling kissed me. Sorry, Fred, if you're out there still! There was nothing wrong with you. I was outraged, because the self-preserving shell I'd built around myself was being invaded. Then later, in high school, when I was about fourteen or fifteen, I was chosen for a part in a play that involved being kissed by a handsome sixth-former. I absolutely hated it. Poor lad, it must have felt like kissing a lump of wood. But his trouble at rehearsals was short-lived. The teacher producing the play eventually dropped me from the cast, and chose the prettier and much more kissable understudy instead! That remained my attitude to boys and men for a number of years: always dreaming of a Mr Knightley ("Emma" was one of our set books for English), but feeling ill-at-ease and horribly unattractive whenever real flesh-and-blood males were around.

One of our family friends did nothing to help. When I was about eighteen, I went to spend a weekend with my sister, who was then working in Leamington Spa. It had been arranged that our parents' friend would pick me up from Leamington and take me home on the Sunday afternoon because he was coming up to Lancashire on business for a few days. To my horror, he wanted me to spend the journey with my hand on his thigh as he drove – and I'd been brought up to be polite and conciliatory to adults. When we finally arrived home and he parked the car, he insisted on kissing me long and hard before we went in to join my parents. I was seething with anger. Later that evening he offered to drive me to college in Manchester the following morning. I refused; quite politely, I thought. "Oh, I'd better stick to my usual routine. I've stuff to read on the train."

But Mum chipped in, "Don't be silly, Joan. He's got to go to south Manchester anyway. He might as well take you."

She should have known better. For some years, Hilary and I had commented that a cool hello or goodbye kiss from this man was likely to become too close a hug. We used to remind one another with a whispered "arch the back" when we offered him a cheek to kiss goodbye. But that day the "good little thing" gave in and accepted the lift in silence.

In later years, I learned to be more outspoken and confrontational, but at that time I had a horror of being impolite. My only refuge was silence.

My eighth birthday

CHAPTER THREE

Growing Up

1951 - 1958

Where was God in all the stresses and strains of my girlhood and adolescence? Did he still seem the tight-lipped disapproving being I'd imagined when I was young?

Well, for a start, life wasn't all stress and strain. Sport at school was a great happiness. In winter, we played hockey. My favourite position was centre half – far enough back to be defensive, far enough forward to feed the ball up to the wings and get us into a position to score. Just once, I scored a goal myself. I came out of a tackle with the ball in my possession, but realised that the forward line wasn't ahead of me; so I raced on with it alone. An opposing defender came to tackle me, but I did a little manoeuvre we'd been practising, drew the ball to my left around her stick and kept on running with it. The next defender got the opposite treatment. The ball was flicked to my right behind her, and I jumped over her stick and ran on to continue dribbling towards the goal. Now only the goalie remained. Her stick was outstretched to her right, but I had only to raise the ball a few inches off the ground to get it over her stick and into the goal. The final score was 1-0 to us. I couldn't believe what I'd done. Especially because our opponents that day were Rochdale Grammar School, and we hardly ever beat them. It wasn't total joy, however, because one of my friends said, "I was just behind you. You should have waited for me." And then I felt I'd been unsporting and a bad team player. But I had got my one and only goal, and now, sixty-odd years later, it's still a pleasure to think of it!

In summer we played tennis, not just at school, but also in the local park whenever we had a free Saturday. We knew a young man called Taffy from our Exclusive Brethren Meeting in Bury, who was a couple of years older than Bryan. Hilary and I had the ambition of beating the two fellows in a doubles game. Most weeks they beat us, as they were older and stronger, but once, just once, we won. They must have hated it! It was good of them to play with us so regularly – it certainly improved my game. At school I was in the first couple of the tennis six, and usually did all right. When losing in a match, however, I was apt to give up and lose all fight. I remember my tennis partner saying to me once in frustration, "Joan, don't be so pathetic." She might have meant "apathetic", but I felt ashamed anyway.

Another of my great joys was literature. My dad had reluctantly given permission for me to stay on in the sixth form, take A-levels and go on to teacher training college. My favourite subject at A-level was English Literature. I loved reading, could get quite emotional over poetry and was thrilled from time to time to go to the theatre. Ah, that was a bit of a problem. In general, Exclusive Brethren did not have radios in their homes and did not go to the cinema or the theatre. One of my maiden aunts never read anything except the Bible, or books about the Bible published by our own Exclusive Brethren publisher; so I was on thin ice. Dad, more broad-minded than most Brethren fathers, allowed us to go on school trips to the theatre, and I rather deceitfully would say, "There's a party from school going to the Library Theatre in Manchester to see a play we're studying," not mentioning that the party from school consisted of just me and a few friends. I loved those evenings.

And I loved the evenings when my parents were out at a Bible study or a prayer meeting and I was left in on my own. Bryan was away doing National Service by the time I was in the sixth form, and Hilary was working in Birmingham and Leamington Spa as a buyer in an up-market firm selling girls' fashions. So there were times when I had the house to myself. My treat was to sit by the kitchen fire, reading a book and eating an apple – or something more calorific! There must have been other homework to do but, when I think of it, I can only remember reading. If there had been no metamorphosis, the person I was then would have lived out her life as an infant teacher, would have weighed about twenty stones, and would have spent her leisure time in a dream world of fiction. But changes were ahead.

The summer when I was seventeen, I had taken my A-levels and was leaving school. In those days, the eleven-plus exam to determine what type of secondary school we went to was not just for eleven-year-olds. It was called the proficiency test and could be taken at any age. So I'd gone to high school at ten years old. By the time I was fifteen and ready to take GCEs, which were replacing the old School Certificate, the system had changed and there *was* an age limit. For that reason, I, together with a few others in my year, went on into the first year sixth a year early. We had to keep up with GCEs, including some different set-books, and study for A-levels at the same time. That challenge, plus the fact that I was finding my feet socially and chatting my way through many a study period, meant that my A-level results were not impressive. But I had passed and was ready to embark on the adult world.

That gave me pause. I wasn't old enough to go to training college – you had to be eighteen for that – so I was planning to work part-time at a school for deaf children in Old Trafford, Manchester. My interests were narrowing down, and I thought that ultimately I might be a teacher for children with some disability, probably deafness. This part-time job would help me to see whether that was truly the way forward for me. But what was this "way forward"? I was beginning to see what job I'd do, but what person would I be? What was to be the motivating force behind my life?

In the context of the world I'd been brought up in, I felt as though I'd either got to commit myself to God, or turn my back on him and walk away – sitting on the fence was no longer an option. I decided to make a commitment. One weekend I sat down at the piano and sang a hymn:

Saviour, while my heart is tender,
I would yield that heart to thee,
All my powers to thee surrender,
Thine and only thine to be.

I had thought I was on my own in the room, but an adopted great aunt of ours was there. "If you can sing that, Joan," she said, "you ought to be breaking bread." (That was the way we expressed our membership of the church – by taking Communion.) For a moment I was almost put off. I didn't want her to think she had influenced me – this was between me and God. But I realised I was being petty. It *was* between me and God, and I did mean it, so I duly asked to "break bread" and was accepted as a fully-fledged sister! As time went on, I realised that becoming a committed Christian wasn't the same as belonging to the Brethren. But at the time it seemed the obvious thing.

In that group of Christians I found myself with all sorts of questions. One that was frequently in my mind and my conversations was, "If what we have is so good, why do we not send out missionaries to share it with the rest of the world?"

"That's not what God is focussing on now," people assured me. "He's working to make his church pure. Numbers aren't important." I listened, but was unconvinced. I had questions too about the restrictions we put on ourselves: restrictions about the sort of clothing thought appropriate for Christians, about us trying to be as uninvolved as possible with the world... I had questions, but I put them to the back of my mind and gave being "a good sister" my best shot.

Hilary, with her job and her interest in fashion, was not so good at toeing the line as I was. One year, when the fashion was for loose, flowing coats, Hilary wore a large, purple winter coat that floated around her as she walked. My Sunday coat was made of greenish Harris tweed with a belt, eminently sensible and sisterly!

Clothes were a bit of a problem. When I was at teacher training college, I lived at home and travelled daily by bus, train and another bus to Didsbury in Manchester. The travelling used up almost all the money that Dad gave me as a weekly allowance. And because I knew how he felt about girls and education, I didn't want to ask for more. I desperately needed some new blouses. Imagine my joy when a relative gave me two new white cotton blouses that had belonged to a deceased friend of hers. I felt that God had arranged it for me. What touched my heart the most was that they were the right size. Imagine that! A God so great that he made the whole universe, yet he knew my size!

Hilary and I shared a passion to do some good in the world. There was a time in our late teens when we used to visit the chronically sick ward of our local hospital once a week. We went in the evening and chatted to some of the old men who were there for a long time. I have forgotten most of them now, but can remember the hands of one old gentleman, distorted with arthritis, pale mauve against the white of the bed sheet, and cold as we gently shook his hand. He always thanked us for coming.

Another of our ventures was making friends with some of the children who lived along the street where our Meeting room was. It was one of the poorest streets in the town and when the doors were open on a hot day, you could smell the houses as you walked past. We got to know some of the children, and were thrilled when they agreed to come to the Sunday evening Gospel Service at the Meeting room. Not everyone was as thrilled as we were, however. Some of the elderly sisters complained that they were covered in fleabites! These activities were somewhat unusual for young sisters. We were supposed to keep quiet and conform.

When I finished training, I got a job teaching the reception class of a local primary school, but was still pursuing my goal of teaching the deaf one day. I happened to mention to one of our friends that I'd heard of a school for the deaf in India, and it was near to a Brethren Meeting of the same group as our own. "I'm thinking of getting a job there one day," I said.

He gave a rather derisive snort and said, "You always sail as close to the wind as you can."

I was amazed. I saw myself as keeping the rules and being "a good sister". But, more importantly, I see now, I was also learning to follow Jesus and to see needy people with his eyes.

Another change that came about in those years was something I was unaware of until I went to the dentist one afternoon for a routine check-up. He asked me if I was a religious person and, when I looked surprised, he explained that he had only three patients who sat in his chair with no sign of nervousness at all. One was a Jewish rabbi, one was a vicar and the third one was me! Remembering the performance I'd put on as a little girl when I'd bitten the hand of the dentist's wife, I could only marvel at the way God changes us when we commit our lives to him. From being a more than usually fearful person, I seemed to be becoming an unusually calm one. Without any effort on my part – amazing!

Eventually I moved on from the Infant School in Bury where I'd started my teaching career. I'd seen an advertisement for a teacher at the Royal School for Deaf Children in Birmingham, who were willing to train someone who didn't already have the qualification for teachers of the deaf. It was just what I'd wanted, but before I sent off the application I got cold feet about leaving home and branching out in a whole new place. "I'm okay where I am," I said. "I don't *have* to teach the deaf."

Dad was unhappy with that. "But you've been talking about it for years."

Mum said to him, "You sound as if you want her to leave home."

Dad's reply was typical of him. With a wise smile he said, "There comes a time when parent birds push the fledglings out of the nest."

He was so right. And to Birmingham I went.

Tennis team

CHAPTER FOUR

Royal School for the Deaf, Birmingham

1958 - 1962

The Deaf School in Edgbaston was an old establishment with a main block, where the children lived, and several large detached houses in a row, which were used as classrooms and rooms to house those of the staff who lived in. The main block was in the last couple of years of its life when I went there. The dormitories were long rooms with rows of metal beds – a typical Victorian charitable institution soon to be replaced with more home-like modern houses. My room was upstairs in one of the other houses. Along the corridor there were four rooms for single teachers and one flat for a married teacher and his family. For our meals we went to a staff dining room in another building. As teachers, our work was mainly in the classroom, but we had some additional supervision duties in the evenings and at weekends. As I settled in my room that first evening I had a sense of excitement, but also some trepidation. Would I cope on my own without the support of my family? I usually prayed sitting up in bed, but this felt important. I knelt on the polished floor by my bed and asked the Lord to help me.

When Sunday came, I duly went to the nearest Meeting, armed with a "letter of commendation" from the Brethren in Bury, telling the Brethren in Harborne that I was "one of us"! The people in the Harborne Meeting were amazing. There were several young adults away from home, like myself – university students, nurses and teachers

– and we were all treated with astonishing kindness and hospitality. In my years there, it became the norm to be booked up every Sunday of the term to spend the day with one or other of the families in the church. The most amazing family were the Robinsons. The father worked in an office for the City Council, I think, the mother was a teacher and there were four children in their teens or early twenties. Their door was always open for others. I have never known more generous, self-sacrificing kindness than they showed us. But it was all with a chat and a laugh – nothing ponderous. One day another young, single woman and I were in the back of their car with one of their girls, when Mr Robinson pulled over and stopped. "Something funny with the lights," he said. "They're pointing up at the sky." It wasn't until the boys started laughing that I realised he was teasing Enid and me – both quite well-built young women!

At school I had a great time. Sometimes I felt almost guilty when I received my salary, because it hadn't felt like work at all. Teaching in an ordinary school had been hard work. A class of thirty children isn't always easy to manage and sometimes the teacher must be a bit of a sergeant major. But a class of deaf children didn't have more than eight or ten pupils, so it felt more like a family, and that suited me better. My best year there was with a group of ten-to-fourteen-year-olds. Their previous teacher had stuck to the letter of the law of the accepted methods of those days: no signing in class – the children had to lip-read and communicate through speech. That method may work well with partially deaf or very able deaf children, but this class were profoundly deaf and not especially bright. The result was that they came into the classroom with glazed eyes, expecting not to understand, expecting to be bored. The headmaster had said to me, "I don't mind what methods you use. Just get them learning again." So we had a ball. We went into Birmingham on the bus one day and bought a cage and a hamster to keep in the classroom. Another time we bought a fish tank and went fishing for tadpoles in Canon Hill Park. Sometimes I invited them to my room to make popcorn on a little gas ring. When Monday morning came and it was time for them to write their routine letter home, they actually had something interesting to say, and their letters were full of illustrations of the adventures we'd been having.

One day I overstepped myself. It was winter and over lunch it had snowed heavily. "Too good a chance to miss," I thought. We abandoned the lessons planned for that afternoon, donned coats, hats and scarves, and went out onto the playing field for a gorgeous half hour of snowballing. Two or three other classes saw us there and came out to join us. Never was there so much laughter and fun... Until the headmaster came out on the terrace and ordered us all back into our classrooms. He wasn't pleased. Nor was the assistant matron when she had to dry a mountain of wet school uniforms. I apologised, of course. But I couldn't truly regret the spontaneity and joy that those institutionalised children had experienced.

I remember each child in that class. One was a shy, quiet little chap of about eleven years old, red-haired and wearing glasses. Going for my lunch one day, I met him in the corridor outside the staff dining room. It was unusual to see a child in that area, and I assumed that he was ill and had been to see the school matron. Our conversation through signs and facial expressions ran something like this:

"What are you doing here?"

"I've been to see matron to get measured up for a new blazer."

"Oh, that's a relief. I thought you were poorly."

"No, I'm okay."

He beamed at me. I patted him on the shoulder. That was all. But down the corridor was the Woodwork teacher, and he had observed the incident.

"I don't agree with what you believe, Joan," he said, "but you've got the most important thing."

"What's that, Ray?"

He was embarrassed, but said it. "You've got love."

I was moved almost to tears. Could it be that this self-centred little girl was actually changing?

Another child in my class was Gillian, profoundly deaf and deeply frustrated by life. One day she came to the teacher's table with a page of beautifully neat sums that she'd just done. But all wrong. I made the mistake of putting a cross by the first couple, and that was enough. She barged out of the room, slammed the door behind her, and went to sit under a tree outside, her head in her hands. I went to sit beside her, but no way was Gillian going to look at me. A deaf person, of course, can't "hear" you unless they're looking at you. Maybe she thought I'd be angry. I don't know. As it happened, anger was the last emotion I was feeling at that moment. Compassion and concern for her and, yes, anger with myself for being such a blundering idiot, not understanding how she would feel. I thought of Francis Thompson's poem "The Hound of Heaven", where the writer has been running from God and refusing to look at him, but realises:

Halts by me that footfall.
Was my gloom after all
Shade of his hand outstretched caressingly?

So I put an arm round Gillian's shoulders. For a moment there was no response. Until a tear ran down her cheek and her hand came up to touch mine. We went back into school together.

One of the boys in that class was Joe. He had come from a Traveller family, and was feisty, aggressive and not yet quite adapted to the ways of school. He often sat daydreaming in class. When I caught his eye, I'd say, "Get on with your work, Joe," and he'd always respond by putting his fists up to me. After this little routine had happened a few times, I decided to call his bluff. I told him to get on with his work, he put up his fists, and I said, with the appropriate gesture, "Come on, then." To everyone's amazement, he did. He marched up to me and punched me hard on the side of my nose! At that moment the bell went for break. I dismissed the class, decided not to go for coffee, and sat down to think about what I ought to do. But there was no time to think. News of Joe punching a teacher had gone round the playground in seconds. Some of the bigger boys had told Joe about the consequences of such an action. And here they were bringing in a very subdued Joe to say sorry. What was I to do? It was my fault after all. I *had* said, "Come on, then." So now I could only say, "Not your fault, Joe," and shake hands to show we were still friends. That was not the end of the story, though. After the break, the senior boys told their teacher, and he came to my classroom to make sure I was all right and to find out what had happened. I lied. For one of the very few times in my adult life I told a blatant lie, and I repeated it several times over the next few days, whenever people commented on my black eye. "Yes," I said, "Joe and I were having an altercation. And I turned round swiftly to the cupboard and hit my face on the cupboard door." It was wrong, I know, but I couldn't take the risk of Joe being punished for something that was really my fault. And Joe? For a couple of weeks, he had to endure seeing my black eye whenever he looked at me and, bless the lad, he became as putty in my hands! No more aggression, no more fists raised!

The other boy I want to tell you about is Frank, a good-looking, red-cheeked, chubby lad. One day the other lads were teasing him and he was looking very embarrassed, so I asked what was going on. They told me that he was Mr Walters' girlfriend. Mr Walters was a teacher in another school in the city, but lived at the Deaf School in exchange for some supervision duties. This was deeply disturbing information. It could have been just a silly joke, or it could have been something a lot more sinister. But it was before the days of child protection policies in schools and I had no idea what to do. Later that day I saw Mr Walters and said, "Walt, I need to talk to you." We went into an empty classroom and I told him what I'd heard, and warned him that if I saw or heard the least whisper of anything like that again, I'd immediately tell the headmaster. Thankfully I didn't have to. In protection of "my" kids, I was becoming bolder, even learning to confront.

But one day I was the one being confronted. A student teacher was spending some weeks in our school. He had been a teacher in a mainstream school for some years, but was now specialising in the education of the deaf and was doing a teaching practice with us. Listening to his conversation in the staff dining room, I realised that he was a keen Christian and I was delighted that he was there. One day, however, he asked me what church I attended, and when I told him that it was Exclusive Brethren, his face fell. "I was afraid of that," he said. How did he guess? I suppose the long hair, unfashionable clothes and prim appearance might have been clues! But why did he feel negative about the Brethren? It turned out that some years previously he and his friends had spent a summer holiday holding evangelistic meetings in the villages of northeast Scotland. Everywhere they went they were welcomed with joy by the local churches – except around the fishing villages of the Moray Firth, where there was a strong Exclusive Brethren tradition. There these eager young Christians had been treated harshly, told they were unwelcome and had been asked to move on. I went away from that conversation ashamed and unsettled.

Chapter Five

Leaving Exclusive Brethren

1961

As the months went on, those feelings of being ill at ease continued. One school holiday, I was at home in Lancashire, and attended a big three-day Brethren conference in the Free Trade Hall in Manchester. The speaker at that conference was an American called Jim Taylor Junior, the son of a James Taylor who had been a well-known Bible teacher among us. But the son was not of the calibre of his father. It seemed as if he took pleasure in introducing fresh legislation, loosely based on a verse of the Bible, and insisting that this was a word from God that we must all obey. And we'd been schooled for years in the concept that what our leaders said must take precedence over our individual conscience. Such a dangerous emphasis – the stuff that cults are made of!

One morning at that three-day Meeting in Manchester, we were studying a passage in one of Paul's letters to the Corinthians. There it says that Christians should not associate with fellow Christians whose lives are blatantly evil, "with such a one not even to eat". And that verse was taken as the basis for a new edict: we must not eat with anyone who was not "one of us". All through the lunch break, groups of distressed and agitated people were talking about it. People were thinking of their own situation with relatives – family members even – who were not members of our group. Surely God can't mean us to shun them and refuse to eat with them... This must have been serious – sisters as well as brothers were in on the discussions!

At the beginning of the afternoon session, someone immediately asked a question about it. "How does what was said this morning fit in with the fact that Jesus's religious opponents accused him of welcoming sinners and eating with them?"

"Ah yes, that was Jesus," Jim Taylor Junior replied, "but we are more prone than he to compromise our purity. There are different instructions for us."

To me, it was like a weight in the pit of the stomach. This was a step too far. If the teaching of our sect of Brethren was going to be given more importance than the teaching of Jesus, I wanted nothing more to do with it. After the holiday, I went back to Birmingham and found that my friends at the Harborne Meeting had heard what had happened in Manchester and some were feeling as I did. That helped. Brethren from the five Meetings in different areas of Birmingham got together in a large hall in the city for Bible studies, and there the atmosphere was very different – very much laying down the law. I couldn't stomach it, and more than once sat quietly reading my bible, ignoring the discussion going on at the front of the hall. Eventually I phoned my dad.

"It's no good," I said. "I can't cope with this any longer. I'm going to leave the Brethren."

He cautioned me, "Think again. Remember how much understanding of the Bible our Brethren had in the past. This nonsense might be just a temporary blip," and so on.

I felt for Dad. Bryan and his young wife, Janet, had already been excommunicated. Their offence was that – as a vet – Bryan was a Member of the Royal College of Veterinary Surgeons and – to the Brethren – membership of anything was anathema. This had been a great grief to my parents. And Dad was ill at the time. So I decided to hang on for Dad's sake.

It cost me something emotionally. Our beliefs were such a huge part of our lives. The Meeting wasn't just where we went on Sunday mornings – it was what we did most evenings as well, the heart of our whole spiritual and social life. So to feel that we had gone wrong was like the walls of our house falling down. But somehow the foundation of the house was still there. God was still there. I prayed daily for him to tell me what to do. And one lunch-break, when I'd decided not to eat but to spend the time praying, I suddenly knew the answer. It was as if God simply said, "It's okay. You can leave now." I immediately wrote a letter to the leading brother in our Harborne Meeting, saying that I was leaving and explaining why.

I went along to the Post Office to mail the letter. There I met Ken, one of our young brothers, a social worker who'd been a friend of Bryan's at university. He told me that, after some weeks of uncertainty, he'd decided to knuckle down and accept the Brethren's teaching. To me, in my new freedom, it seemed disastrous. I said, "When we die and meet God face-to-face, we can't shelter behind the Brethren then. It's us individually and God... What can we say to him then?" I mentioned George Bernard Shaw's play about Joan of Arc, where Joan, bewildered by the teaching of the Catholic Church at that time, says, "What judgement can I judge by but my own?" I told him that I'd decided to follow my own conscience and leave. As I remember this now, it seems as if I was being hard on Ken, a highly intelligent, sensitive young man, schooled – as we'd all been – for many years that holding our own individual views was a form of pride. But my heart bled for him, and it was a great joy to me, years later, to know that he and his wife were finally free of that system and happily worshipping in a Church of England.

That evening, I phoned my parents to tell them. Dad picked up the phone. This time, when I told him what I'd decided, he said, "That's astonishing. Just this week, I've come to the same decision. I shan't go to the Meetings anymore." My heart sang. This time I wasn't adding to his grief. Mum was not a problem. She had never been as convinced as Dad was, and had always had a big heart for those outside the Brethren as well as those within the sect.

From the Brethren's point of view, my letter wasn't the end of the story. Two of the brothers from Harborne arranged to see me, one of them our dear Mr Robinson. He mentioned that his younger daughter had seen me the day before among a crowd of shoppers in New Street while she was on a bus.

He'd asked her, "Did Joan still look like a sister?"

And she had said, "She looked like a Christian."

He was amused to tell me that. I could not think of any other way I'd prefer to look!

But that evening, in that context, they were on official business and had to toe the party line. They assured me of the love of the Brethren for me and encouraged me to stay. But I couldn't. My whole being, my whole experience of God, was contrary to the increasing narrowness and legalism of the system I'd been brought up in. The God I was getting to know was all for abundant life; the route the Brethren were on was a crushing of life, a route to deadness. And hadn't God said to me, "It's okay. You can go now."? I sat there crying with my nose running and, for some reason, without a handkerchief! The wrench was hard, but I knew it was necessary.

The interview was followed a few days later by an Assembly Meeting, a gathering at the big hall in the city to formally withdraw from me. People couldn't have been kinder. Again they pleaded with me to stay. Then someone said, "You're allowed to respond, Joan" – the one and only time that I, as a woman, was permitted to speak out in a Meeting!

"Thank you for the amazing love and hospitality you've shown me in my years in Birmingham. I know I shall never forget it. But for me, feeling as I do the wrongness of an increasing emphasis on separation from the world, it would be hypocrisy to stay."

Nobody spoke.

I whispered to the person next to me, "Do I go out now?"

"I think so."

And I left – again in tears.

One of our rules was that when someone leaves they are not contacted or spoken to again. What I did was going to cut all those friends totally out of my life. I knew I'd miss them. But as I walked out of the door, Hilary was waiting for me in the dark street outside. She drove us to a wooded park where we walked for a while. I remember saying to her, "One of the brothers said that if I left them, I'd be leaving God. Am I?"

"Not necessarily," she replied. "It's up to you."

At that time she was still a member of a Brethren Meeting, so what she did in keeping close to me was a heroic stand against what we'd been taught, and it had to be kept secret. After our walk, we went back to my room at school and had cups of tea. Hilary insisted on waiting until I was bathed and in bed and then, late that evening, set off to drive back from Birmingham to Manchester where she was living. What a sister!

The next morning, there was a postcard on the shelf by the front door of the house where my room was. It was addressed to "Saint Joan". On the other side in Ken's neat writing was the quote from Bernard Shaw: "What other judgement can I judge by but my own?"

What was I going to do next? I carried on living and working at the Deaf School, enjoyed the freedom of not having Meetings most evenings, and tried to think what to do the next Sunday. Near the Deaf School, hidden behind trees, on the corner of a quiet road, was a Quaker Meeting House. I'd passed it many times and thought what a peaceful place it looked. So the first empty Sunday morning, that's where I went. It was a small group of people and we sat quietly for most of the hour. One lady got to her feet and read something, but in the main we sat in silence. At the end, people were friendly and welcoming, and two ladies invited me to go to tea one day after school. That was so lovely of them. They encouraged me to talk about myself, and asked if I had any questions about the Quaker faith. The two things I remember asking were seriously important to me then, and have been significant in the years since: "Do you work together with other Christians?" and, "Do you send out missionaries to take the good news to the rest of the world?" Those were the issues at the top of my mind, but not at the top of the minds of those two lovely ladies. I didn't go back to that little church.

On the Sunday evening, I couldn't help it, I went back to the Brethren Meeting at Harborne, arrived at the last minute, sat on the back row, and left the moment the service was over. I knew nobody would speak to me. But one person did. One of the Robinson boys hared along the road after me and caught up with me at the bus stop.

"I'm not letting you go with no-one speaking to you," he said.

"Oh, thank you, thank you. But go back. You'll get into awful trouble."

He had to go. Years later, I met him and his wife and family, by then members of a much freer type of Brethren. I was so glad they hadn't stayed where we all were.

One problem that was bothering me was what to do with my summer holiday. Hilary and I had been planning a holiday together, but while I was "out" and she was still "in" she couldn't get away with it.

Another problem was which church to settle in. I could only try a few and see if one felt right. And another question mark was hanging over my long-term future. This missionary thing – what was that all about?

One Saturday morning, I went into Birmingham and, with some hesitation, braved the CLC Christian bookshop, at that time near Snow Hill Station. It was a whole new experience for me, because in the past I'd only ever read Christian books written by Exclusive Brethren. Was I about to fall into heresy? I spent ages looking around, but I think I bought only a Christian weekly newspaper. However, I saw a poster advertising a Birmingham rally for young Christians. It was to be held in the town hall that night and I decided to go. I must have looked rather odd in the casual free-and-easy atmosphere of that rally. I had gone on my Lambretta scooter but when I parked it and took off my helmet, I combed my dishevelled hair and carefully put on a blue linen hat with a brim. Years of habit were not going to be broken easily! The main event of the evening was the showing of a Wycliffe Bible Translators film about mission work in a South American tribe. One shot was of the feet of a woman missionary – she had been walking through the forest and come to a stream that had to be crossed, so, with bare feet and a hiked-up skirt, was picking her way through the water. Something in me responded, "I'll go there if you want me to, Lord."

The Christian newspaper I'd bought included an advert for the Mission to Miners. A tent mission was to be held in August, in a mining town in the north of France. A team of young Christians was needed to help. Some ability to speak French would be an advantage. Applications to...

I applied.

Chapter Six

Adjusting to the Wider Christian World

1961 et al.

I was very uncertain whether my French-speaking ability would be an advantage at all. I had passed A-level French, but my spoken French lagged way behind what I could read or write. Hilary and I had been on a camping holiday in France the previous year, but Hilary nearly always said what was needed while I was still working out what tense of the verb was required! She was still a braver soul than I, and not a bit daunted by the thought that she might be making mistakes.

However, minimal spoken French or not, I was accepted and duly arrived in Courrières for the start of the mission. A team of four of us were staying at the home of the missionaries, who were a couple from Birmingham with two small children. After our meal on the first evening, it was agreed that we have a time of prayer together about the coming weeks. To my utter horror, I realised that women as well as men were praying, and that as one after another around the circle were praying, it was getting close to my turn. I had *never* prayed audibly before. You remember about "women keeping silence in the church"? Sweating and stammering, I managed a few sentences. What the others thought, I shall never know. They were Bible College students, missionaries in training. I must have seemed a fish out of water to them.

One of our jobs was to go round the streets and houses of the town inviting people to the evangelistic meetings in the marquee. One evening

I gave my carefully practised invitation to a group of men on a street corner. The full-time missionary was following some way behind, and had a quick chat with them too. When he caught up with us, he was smiling. The men had said to him that the young woman had spoken French just like it ought to be spoken, but – as he saw me beginning to look rather pleased with myself – he added that their French-speaking ability was limited. They had arrived in France from North Africa only a couple of days before!

When the missionary and his wife learned that I was working at a school in Edgbaston, they said, "You must be near Birmingham Bible Institute." If so, I'd never heard of it! "When you get back, pop down and see Mr and Mrs Bonsall, the principal and his wife, and give them our love."

A few weeks later, back in Birmingham, I found the BBI houses and timidly rang the doorbell. The principal himself opened the door. I don't think I remembered to give him the message from the couple in Courrières. I just found myself blurting out, "I want to be a missionary. How do I go about it?"

With typical enthusiasm, Mr Bonsall replied, "Term starts next week. Come and join us."

I couldn't do that, of course. I was committed to the Deaf School for another year, but BBI did evening classes and I started going to some of those. Some of them were astonishingly good. We had a series on the Old Testament by a visiting lecturer – H.L. Ellison, from a Jewish background. This wasn't the sort of narrow, focussed-on-us teaching I'd heard before. This was the amazing story of a mighty God working out his plans through the sweep of human history. I lapped it up hungrily.

But don't imagine that Bible College students are an unsmiling, frighteningly earnest class of people. Yes, they were earnest, but there was lots of laughter too. One evening, at the end of the lecture, I came out to go back to school on my Lambretta, but could not find my crash helmet anywhere. Two or three kind people were helping me search the hallway and the steps outside, when we noticed smirks going round some of the young fellows. "Try the road outside," they said, and there, hanging from a lamppost, was my missing helmet! One of the culprits was a young man from Northern Ireland called Philip Kearney.

He started coming with one or two other students to help with a Sunday school class at the Deaf School that I held for the children who hadn't gone home for the weekend. And it was there, one week, that I had one of the most memorable experiences of my life. I was talking to the children about Jesus being like a shepherd, and us being like the sheep that he looks after. I had bought some little metal badges with a picture of the Good Shepherd on them and, during the course of the afternoon, gave a badge to several children who answered a question or did anything particularly well. Later, as the children were leaving, I noticed a little Traveller girl. I had heard her story: because of her deafness, she had been hidden at the back of a caravan and only recently come to the attention of the authorities, so was now suffering the trauma of being sent to a boarding school. On arrival, she had been taken by the assistant matron to have a bath before she was kitted out in her new school uniform – and had struggled and screamed throughout the process. You can imagine how she felt. She had no language to ask what was happening to her, and no language to understand any explanation. She must have been terrified. Now, as she filed out from Sunday school with the other children, she looked beseechingly at me. Suddenly I knew what she wanted. There was a Good Shepherd badge left on the table. As I picked it up and pinned it on her uniform, I felt the flood of God's love go through me to that little girl. I pinned the badge on her. She smiled. That was all. But that moment gave me an unforgettable glimpse of the overwhelming understanding and compassion of God for every human being.

Other people had left Exclusive Brethren around the same time as I had. One of them was Miss Lewis, an elderly lady who lived in sheltered housing in Quinton, beyond Harborne. From time to time over the years I had popped in to see her or she had come to have tea with me in my room at school. Now, I continued to visit her. One day we were talking about the need we both felt to find another church, and she asked me to go with her to a little church just down the road from where she lived. The next Sunday we went there together. I don't think she liked it very much, but it suited me well. It was an Evangelical Free Church, simple in style but sincere, eager to serve God, and Bible-based in its teaching. From then on, I made that my regular church.

I'd been going there for a few months when, one Sunday in the middle of a sermon on quite a different topic, I found myself thinking about baptism. In our particular group of Exclusive Brethren, the custom had been to baptise babies of Christian parents – not by sprinkling but by immersion! Baptisms were performed in the bath of the parents' home. The baby was swished through the water headfirst so that the water wouldn't go up the baby's nose, and everyone prayed for the little one to grow up and come to personal faith in Jesus. Now, however, I began to see baptism as an act of commitment by someone who has already come to faith, and I wondered if it would be possible for me to go through another act of baptism, as I embarked on a whole new phase of my life with God. It was possible and a date was fixed. I invited my parents to come, but at the time, Dad wasn't willing. He felt that he had baptised me as a baby, sincerely entrusting me to God, and that my wanting to be baptised again was somehow a denial of what had been meaningful to him. I understood that, accepted that they weren't coming and invited instead a couple of fellow teachers, Gordon and Margaret. To my joy, they came, and Margaret even made a celebratory cake for us to eat when we got back to school. Gordon found the atmosphere strange at my new church, with the warm moist air from the baptistery and the chink of teacups. Not quite the formality that he was used to in church! Margaret had been amused by one thing. The custom after an adult baptism was for a friend to hold a large towel so that the person coming up out of the water could be wrapped in it for warmth, and to modestly cover the wet clinging clothes. But baptism, like life, is a thing you do only once and don't have a chance to practise! I forgot the bit about the towel and made a beeline for the door with Mrs Round and the towel in hot pursuit like a matador after a bull!

Mr and Mrs Round were the leaders of that church at Quinton, a godly, unassuming couple to whom I owe a great debt. When, the next year, I left teaching and became a full-time student at BBI, they prayed for me every day, and that continued in the years that followed. They also encouraged the church to support me financially. They were faithful, generous people with a great heart for God's mission throughout the world.

Since I was already attending some lectures at BBI, I was beginning to make friends with some of the full-time students. One was Mary, a girl from a difficult background, but with a real longing to serve God. She came to tea with me one Sunday in my room at school. In the course of conversation, she mentioned that she was having trouble finding the money for her college fees, and when I expressed shock and dismay at that, she said confidently, "Not to worry. My Father owns the cattle on a thousand hills." This was a new world I was beginning to move in, a world where you do what God wants and trust him to provide what you need. As time went on, this became the norm for me too – in the years ahead I had many experiences of what seemed like miraculous provision of finances and other things – but that day I was taken aback by what Mary said.

After tea she took me to Graham Street Elim Church, my first experience of a Pentecostal Church. And for the first time, I heard someone "speaking in tongues". It happens when someone, under the influence of the Holy Spirit, speaks out words that are not in a language they know. They have the emotion of what they are saying – praise or lament, joy or warning – but they don't necessarily know the detail. Sometimes another person in the congregation is given an interpretation of the tongue, and will speak it out for everyone to understand. That evening at Graham Street, although the phenomenon was new to me, I had the conviction that what was being said was for me, and I was sitting on the edge of my seat with anticipation, waiting for the interpretation. When it came, it was a message of comfort and encouragement from God, something like, "You are disappointed. You think that your prayers have not been heard. But I have heard. Keep on praying. Carry on trusting. I am the God who hears you." There was a particular problem that I'd been praying about for a while and, yes, I had been disappointed, but now was utterly reassured. God was listening. I began to feel that my future was quite safe in his hands.

CHAPTER SEVEN

Birmingham Bible Institute

1962 - 1965

I left the Deaf School and, after the summer holidays, moved to become a full-time student at BBI. It was 1962. I was twenty-six, one of the older students, and used to having my own space. At BBI I wasn't going to have a room of my own. I wasn't going to have domestic staff to clean up after me. I wasn't going to be given a liberal cheque at the end of each month. This was a different way of life. The Lambretta I'd had for some time was getting old and constantly needing repair. I realised that I wouldn't be able to afford garage bills any longer. But to my relief, Philip Kearney came to the rescue and offered to do repairs for me if, in exchange, he could make use of the scooter too. BBI students were great at sharing and helping one another out.

The college was housed in several large old houses on the Calthorpe Estate in Edgbaston. Most had been built in Victorian times on land owned by the estate, and had been given a hundred-year lease. Now these leases were running out, and the houses had a very low sale value or were available for short-term rental at a charge that even BBI could afford! The rooms were huge. One term I shared a bedroom with six other young women, a bunk in one corner and five single beds, each with a little space between them for a chair or a small chest of drawers.

I arrived early at the beginning of term, planning to choose a bed in one corner and have my own area. I was too early. Mr Bonsall had been painting the chest of drawers, and as I unpacked my things and opened a drawer to put them away, drips of paint fell down into the drawer! I got my corner, however, and was pleased about that. Then, a couple of weeks later, we were woken in the night by drops of water falling onto our beds from a leaking tank in the roof, and had to shift our beds to the other end of the room. When it was all repaired and dried out and we re-arranged the furniture, I'd lost my corner. I felt as if God had meant that to happen. He didn't like the selfish way I'd chosen the best space for myself. Unlike some other Bible Colleges, BBI was quite basic and disorganised, but we were assured that is was all "GMT", good missionary training. And it was. For me, from my fairly comfortable and rather correct background, it was brilliant training.

I wasn't a very good timekeeper – I still am not! But at BBI ten thirty lights out *meant* ten thirty, and I had to struggle to conform. One night I was still in the bathroom at ten thirty-five and came back to our room in total darkness. There wasn't a whisper. Surely they couldn't all be asleep already. As I tiptoed down the room to my bed, I kicked a metal wastepaper bin, stumbled over a pile of books, wondered why there were so many pairs of shoes in the middle of the floor and got back to a bed that was all disarranged. That's when I started to giggle and was answered by suppressed laughter from the other beds. They'd thoroughly enjoyed hearing me clatter and bump my way through the assault course they'd prepared! But the laughter had to be suppressed – there was usually a tutor on duty to make sure we were all keeping the rules.

Another term, when I was studying for an external exam, I had the luxury of a room in the attic with a sloping roof and space for just two beds. Between the beds, below a roof window, there was room for a ramshackle desk. It was peaceful up there with views of the sky.

Most lectures were in a large area on the ground floor of one of the houses, where two rooms had been made into one. In the summer, the French windows were open to the big old garden, and the room was warm and sunny. In winter, it was heated by a coke stove that got extremely hot. One day when Mr Bonsall was teaching and walking up and down as he spoke, the hem of his academic gown must have stayed for a few seconds on the stove and it began to smoulder. Quite a dramatic interruption to the lecture: "Mr Bonsall, your gown's on fire!"

Another memory of that room is not a pleasant one. One of our tutors was teaching us Old Testament history, and we were thinking about the life of King David. We came to the story of David's adultery with Bathsheba and his subsequent arranging that her husband should die in the heat of battle. I could hardly believe it when the lecturer treated the story in a nudge-nudge wink-wink way, as if adultery was a joke. To me, that story is a heart-breaking account of how a good man can fail his God. Afterwards, I had to tell the lecturer how I felt. I said that I was so shocked by his attitude and that if he continued similarly the next week, I would walk out of the lecture. It wasn't something I spoke about to anyone else, so I got some bemused looks from other students when he began the lecture the following week by saying, "I've got to be careful what I say, or we'll have Miss Boswood walking out." That's not a good memory for me, but I'm glad I was getting a bit bolder as the years went on.

Other members of the staff at BBI were wonderful people. They worked there because they felt that God wanted them there, with long hours, difficult conditions and minimal wages. And some of them, by their teaching and example, have had an impact for good far beyond the walls of BBI, as their students have gone to work in many different situations around the world. One such couple were Bassee and Joyce Kingdon. They were wardens of one of the student houses and I was in their house for a number of terms. One half-term break in May, I was planning to go home to my parents who now lived in Essex, and I was especially looking forward to it because it was going to be my birthday. I hadn't enough money for the petrol I'd need for the Lambretta, but fully expected that before Friday came I'd have what I needed. But Friday arrived and there was no letter in my pigeonhole, no pound note found lurking in a pocket. There was nothing for it but to stay in Birmingham. So I went to Mrs Kingdon and just said, "I'm changing my plans, if that's okay. Could I stay in the house here over the weekend?"

"That's all right," she answered, "as long as you look after yourself."

As we were chatting, her husband came into the room. "Bassee," she said, "have we any money?"

He took out of his pocket a small handful of silver, and separated some that was for the children's dinner money at school.

"Can we give the rest to Joan?" she asked. And without any questions, he gave it to me.

I thanked them profusely and left to pack a few things, head for a petrol station and travel to Essex. It wasn't a lot of money, and Essex was quite a journey away, but the petrol was enough. As I was turning into the little driveway of my parents' house, the engine spluttered and stopped.

Years later I was telling this story to my colleague in Brazil. She asked how I got back from Essex and I was able to say that I'd had gifts of money for my birthday. Then she said, "Oh so you'd be able to pay them back for their kindness," and I was disturbed to realise that I couldn't remember having ever paid them back. I had a chequebook with me in the forest so I wrote a cheque, put a letter with it and, the next time the boat came by, off it went to repay my debt with interest. A while later a reply came. For a number of years, the Kingdons had supported a needy child overseas, sent money every quarter, and prayed daily for this child along with their own two children at home. Money was very, very tight, but each quarter something would happen. Mrs Kingdon would be asked to do some supply teaching for a few days or someone would send them a gift. They had never failed in their quarterly payment. Until this particular time. No opportunities for supply teaching. No unexpected gifts. But out of the blue, from the Amazon forest, came a letter and the repayment of a debt. What a thrill for them! And for me!

Not all lectures at BBI were held in the big lecture room. A small group of us studying New Testament Greek met in Mr Bonsall's study one evening a week and stood round his desk for a couple of hours. One night he was unusually sleepy. It was his habit to get up very early in the morning and spend hours praying for each of the current students and for those who had completed their time at college now working in churches and missions all over the world. By the middle of the evening, he had already had a long, long day. So he said to us, "Take a break for ten minutes, and I'll go upstairs and lie on my bed."

Part of the house was used as a hostel for women students, so I knew my way around. "Come on, folks," I said. "Let's get a cup of tea and some toast." I couldn't imagine that a ten-minute break was going to be nearly enough for him, twenty minutes maybe... But after ten minutes, when we'd barely got our teeth into the toast, there he was in the doorway, bright as a button, reinvigorated, and we had to abandon our snack and get back to Greek!

His life of prayer was well known in the college. Once, saying grace before the evening meal, he remembered his cat at home, which was just producing a litter of kittens. "Lord, thank you for this food and all your provision for us. And Lord, please bless Tibby Brash." Frequently, in the midst of any conversation, he would say, "Word of prayer," bow his head for a moment and ask God's help for the person or situation under discussion. Once, years later, my parents met him at the Keswick Convention and politely introduced themselves. They were surprised at his reaction: "Word of prayer. Lord, bless Joan today in the forest of Brazil. And one day, Lord, please give her a husband." God's blessing wasn't in question, my parents thought, but a husband...? That was perhaps a bridge too far for their faith to go!

One special prayer of Mr Bonsall's was talked about a lot during the time we were students. I'm quoting here from "Running for Revival", a biography of Harry Brash Bonsall, written by his daughter, Ruth McGavin.

> *On one particular occasion Norman Gidney, one of Harry's good friends and financial advisers, was going to an appointment in New Street, Birmingham. As it was raining, he locked his car and made a dash for the building across the road. In his haste, he bumped into a man who was walking briskly in the pouring rain, wearing a grey overcoat and a black homburg hat. Norman immediately apologised – at which point the two men recognised each other.*
>
> *"Brash, how lovely to see you," he said. Harry, the taller of the two, put his arm round Norman's shoulders and promptly said, "Let's have a brief word of prayer."*
>
> *Norman was understandably a little embarrassed standing in the middle of New Street in Birmingham in the pouring rain, with Harry's arm around his shoulders, about to be prayed for! But as Norman loved him and had such tremendous respect for him, there was no way he could resist his request, so Harry began to pray. At which point, Harry being slightly taller bent his head forward and the water which had*

accumulated in the upturned brim of his black homburg poured down Norman's neck – an experience of water baptism which he took without a murmur, though still embarrassed about what was taking place!

Harry's prayer was very short and ended with the phrase "...and Lord, will you please protect Norman from high voltage cables. Amen." The two men gave each other a hug, and Norman ran into the building extremely uncomfortable and very wet.

When he went home that night, Norman relayed the story to his wife. She was highly amused. "Brash is finally losing his marbles," said Norman. "He prayed that I should be protected from high voltage cables!" However, the following Saturday morning, a Sunday School party came to spend the day at Norman's farm in Warwickshire. In order to get their bus through the gates of the farm courtyard, Norman had to take a broom and climb on to an iron gate to lift a sagging telephone cable. The cable ran right across the gate, so he lifted it up with the broom for the coach to come in. He was wearing a large straw hat, which he hardly ever wore, when something knocked the hat off his head as he stood there on the iron gate. Norman looked up with horror, and went cold with the recollection of Harry's prayer, as it was a high voltage cable that had knocked off his hat. Wearing that hat had saved his life, as the iron gate on which he was standing would have been a most powerful earthing of a very high current. It took Norman a long time to get over the shock and miracle of the experience.

We students may have smiled at Mr Bonsall's "words of prayer", but we could not doubt that they were inspired by God and heard by God.

As students, we were all encouraged to pray, too. There was a college service every morning, when we prayed for that day, for old students, and for national and international problems. Groups of students planning to go to similar areas of work would meet once a week in the Africa prayer group, South America prayer group and so on. Because of that Wycliffe Bible Translators film I'd seen, I had a special interest in South America and went along fairly regularly to that prayer group. We met after lunch in the early afternoon. One time, a missionary on home leave from Brazil came to speak to us. Her name was Sheila Tremaine and she was learning the language of the Rikbaktsa tribe. She described the situation there: remote from any town, several days' journey by rubber-tappers' boat up one of the tributaries of the Amazon, the air thick with "piums" – small, biting gnats... I remember thanking God that the situation was already staffed. Even if I did ultimately go to Brazil, I wouldn't be needed in that tribe to cope with those insects.

And we were encouraged to pray on our own. I had a phase when I woke early each day and, ever on the quest for a bit of peace and quiet, hid myself away in a tiny box-room I'd discovered. Apart from a pile of mattresses, the room was empty. I'd get in there, shut the door behind me and lean against the door thinking, "Goodbye, world. Hello, God." I loved that little room. It was there that I first asked God to fill me with his Spirit. I'd had something of a barrier against that experience, having a natural shrinking from anything extreme or over the top. But it was dawning on me that if God was willing to give me a gift, any gift, I'd be an idiot not to accept it. So I came to God, saying sorry for thinking myself too rational and balanced to want the fullness of his Spirit, and asked him to give me all that he wanted to. There was no dramatic change – maybe I'm just not a dramatic person – but from that time onwards I do sometimes find myself praying in tongues, especially when I don't have words to express the emotions I feel, and I have found myself becoming a more peaceful, less-afraid person. Nowadays, I frequently ask God for more of his Spirit, more of his character, as well as more of his power.

At the end of each academic year there was a speech day and prize-giving in one of the halls in the centre of Birmingham. One year the speaker was a certain Gladys Aylward. She is known for the film "The Inn of the Sixth Happiness", which tells of her adventures as a missionary in China. She may have been small, but she was dynamite. She stood in front of a hall full of typical British Christians of that day, and gave us a good telling off. She talked about our comfortable lifestyle, and our obsession with having a nice home with an up-to-the-minute three-piece suite... She made us feel very small. I wasn't surprised, when I heard of her death some years later, to know that she had taken a fatal pneumonia through giving her blanket to a family of beggars in China. She certainly practised what she preached. I'm so grateful that I had the chance to hear that tiny mighty woman of God.

Being obsessed with comfort was not an immediate problem for most of us students. What we needed was to get the right balance between coping with poverty if God wanted that for us and rejoicing in his generosity if we had a time of abundance. At one time I very much needed a new pair of brown shoes, something casual and comfortable that wouldn't look ridiculous on the Lambretta, but tidy enough to wear with my nice suit if I was speaking in a church. One day, on my way home to Essex again, I'd had a lift as far as Ilford and, waiting there for a bus for the rest of my journey, saw just the shoes I needed in a shop window in a sale. I hummed and hawed and examined my conscience about whether I really needed them, until it was time for my bus and I had to leave without them. As I sat on the bus, I had the impression that God wasn't pleased with my asceticism. It was as if he was saying, "Actually, I'd put those shoes there just for you" – but I'd turned my back and left it too late.

Sometime later, back at BBI, we had a chores afternoon, all of us detailed to do some domestic task of cleaning or maintenance around the houses. I came back to my room and noticed, as I thought, someone else's shoes under my bed. I took them round the house: "Has anyone lost a pair of shoes?"

In the end, one of my fellow students came after me embarrassedly along the landing. "I put them there, Joan. Will they fit you? I've been too extravagant and bought two pairs. Can you make use of them?"

They fit me, they were brown, and they were casual-smart – just what I needed. Yes, those years at BBI were a wonderful training ground for the years ahead.

Sadly, in the last term or so of my three years there, BBI went through a time of upheaval. A number of the students were unhappy with some aspects of the running of the college and tried to express their views to the staff. If, at that stage, the staff had listened and there had been some open discussion, a positive way forward could have been found. But instead, a member of the BBI council, someone we didn't know, was asked to speak to the students. It was a brave thing for him to do because, in his view, the students were in rebellion! He talked to us for quite a time, telling us that God had called the staff and leaders to their task (we didn't doubt that) and that our role was to be submissive and grateful. But why could we have no input into trying to make it a better college? When he finished speaking, John, one of my fellow students in the Greek class, stood up and quietly said that he felt there were some things that needed improving in the organisation of the college. He invited those of us who agreed with him to stand. I stood, and so did the majority of the students there. Then we quietly sat down again. No revolt, no anger.

How wise is the proverb, "A gentle answer turns away wrath"! If the council member and the staff had been able to say, "Thank you, John. Bring two or three other students to the next staff meeting with some constructive ideas for us to discuss. We'll see how God leads us to make some changes" – if that had happened the outcome could have been a good one. But no. In my view at that time, John was treated badly. He was told that he would not receive a BBI diploma, in spite of three years of faithful work and study. I could not accept that. I went to the principal and to Mrs Kingdon, my tutor. I said that if John wasn't going to receive his diploma, I didn't want mine either. I had stood with John at the meeting with the council member so if that was a wrong thing to do, I was equally guilty. Mrs Kingdon was sad about it. She told me that I'd been chosen to get the prize for the best leaving student – wow, that was a shock! – but of course, that would not happen now. My parents were coming for the annual speech day celebration and staying in a hotel overnight to transport some of my stuff home – there's only so much that you can carry on a Lambretta! For their sake, I was sorry not to be marching up to get my diploma and that prize. For my sake, it didn't matter. The actual piece of paper was not as valuable to me as all the experience I'd had and all the lessons I'd learned. But it was a sad, sad ending to a wonderful three years.

BBI staff and students

Chapter Eight

Joining Wycliffe Bible Translators
1965

When I began my course at BBI, I thought I would stay for only two years. I was already one of the older ones there, and didn't want to become one of those eternal students! However, one thing seemed to point to the need for a three-year course. I felt more and more drawn to Wycliffe Bible Translators. Wycliffe work in many countries of the world, and have a specific calling to people who, so far, have no translation of the Bible in their own language. Imagine if we had to learn German or Japanese before we could understand the truth about God. We wouldn't do it, would we? It would seem as if God was only interested in foreigners, not us. And that's how it seems to speakers of many minority languages in the world today. Wycliffe members want God to speak in every language! I've always been interested in languages, in spite of my mediocre results in A-level French. And, of course, working with deaf children had increased my awareness of language learning and the complexities of forming the different sounds in a language. It began to seem as if that was the way I should go.

I mentioned it one day when talking to a BBI staff member, and was told that Wycliffe was quite an academic mission so I'd probably benefit from having a degree. How about staying at BBI for three years and aiming to get a Bachelor of Divinity? The idea seemed good to me and I became part of the little group studying New Testament Greek and the Philosophy of Religion – things that wouldn't have been included in the two-year course. I can't say I was very proficient in either of those topics, but I picked up enough to find it useful in the years since.

In the summer of each year, I went to a school run by Wycliffe called the Summer Institute of Linguistics (SIL). These schools were run in former army camps, so the environment was not plush, but there was a happiness, purposefulness and camaraderie as people from all over Europe came together for six or twelve weeks of study and practice. The six-week course was to help people learn a language, any language: how to get your tongue around difficult sounds that don't occur in your mother tongue, how to practise again and again the construction of sentences in the target language, how to sound like a native speaker... The twelve-week course went on to give special help to people who expected to learn, analyse and translate into a language that had never been written down before – a language where grammar books and dictionaries did not yet exist. At the end of the six weeks and again during the twelve-week course, there would be practical times of language learning, when we worked in small groups, getting a taste of someone's language, finding out how to greet people and hold a simple conversation. The highest accolade came from one African student, who in England had hardly any opportunity to hear his own language. After a week teaching us, he said, "I can't believe it. You sound just like women from my home village!" Then we knew that the system worked and our practice had paid off.

While I was at SIL the first summer, I took a set of application papers to apply to become a missionary with Wycliffe. I filled in what I could and took the papers back to the office. David Bendor-Samuel was there.

"Have you any questions?" he asked.

"Only that I'm not a hundred per cent sure that this is what God wants. How can I know?"

"If you're not sure, don't leave the papers here," was David's advice. "God can make you certain when the time is right."

I felt really disappointed by that setback, and the following Sunday evening found a quiet classroom on the camp to think, read my Bible and pray. I "happened" upon a passage in Ezekiel about some prophets who went and prophesied without God having sent them. Their punishment was severe – God said that he was against them. And I was preparing to go and work as a missionary without any certainty that it was God sending me. What a nerve! I saw myself as a cheeky little upstart pushing myself forward without waiting for God's specific call. For the first time in my life, I knew that I deserved hell. I'd often felt useless and unworthy before, but this was different. I saw in myself the human pride and independence that makes us think we can manage without God. He had been hard at work for a number of years, building my confidence, but he didn't want my confidence to be in myself. I had to trust him and wait for his say-so.

Back in Birmingham after the summer, I spoke to the leaders of the little church in Quinton, and asked them to pray about my future. I told them I was very interested in Wycliffe Bible Translators and asked them to let me know if they felt that it was God's will for me. I asked my parents too. Mum said that they had been astonished all along that I should be even thinking of working overseas. "Now, if it had been Hilary, it would make more sense. She's always been much more adventurous than you are! But you must work it out for yourself. You do what you think right."

Some weeks later, the leaders at Quinton had their answer for me. "Sorry, Joan. We are not all happy about you joining Wycliffe." So that was that. For the time being there was nothing more to do except soldier on with my studies at BBI and wait for further instructions from God. I tried to be open to other missions and other areas of the world. But it was always language, Bible translation and South America that seemed to fire my imagination.

Months later I spoke once more to the leaders of the church at Quinton. "I'm so sorry to ask you again. But could you please pray again about whether God wants me in Wycliffe Bible Translators? I'm still feeling that's the right way to go." Bless them, they took it seriously and, wonderfully, they came back this time with a positive answer. Another hurdle crossed.

I got another set of application papers and began to fill them in. It is quite a mammoth effort – there is a great deal of detail required in applying to an overseas mission. Obviously they want to know your history and your abilities, but they also need to know your spiritual experience, your theological views and whether you're the sort of person who can adapt to life in a totally different culture. I heard of one applicant who was so irritated with the amount of information required that he wrote on the bottom of his papers, "P.S. My aunt also has a budgerigar"! I don't know the rest of his story, whether the personnel office staff were amused at his humour or annoyed by his frivolity!

I was filling in these papers again back at the Summer Institute of Linguistics for a second year course. That was another summer of transition. As you know, I'd left BBI without a diploma, but any day we were expecting the results of our London University BD, the external exam I'd been working for. John and Ian were other BBI students at SIL that year. I had a cousin who was working in London who had agreed to go to London University, find the list of external students who had gained a BD, and phone the SIL camp to tell us whether our names were on the list. Remember, this was before the days of mobile phones. My cousin would phone and leave a message at the office, staff there would call us over the tannoy, and we would go to the office to be told what the message was. On the day when our results were due, we heard nothing all morning. We checked with the office, but no – no message had come for any of us. The others were doing their first year course, and had classes that afternoon. As a second year student, I had more free time for private study, so I decided to go up to London myself and find out how we had all done. I was walking from the camp into Merstham to catch the train, when John came cycling along behind me. "The message has come," he said. "I'm so sorry, Joan. They said that Ian and John have passed." I thanked him for coming to tell me and save me wasting time and money going to London. He pedalled madly to his class, and I walked disconsolately back.

Some half-hour later, I was lying on my bed thinking about my life: no diploma, no BD, no certainty that Wycliffe would accept me. "Not much of a life to offer to you, Lord," I said, "but here it is and it's yours if you can do something with it."

There came a knock on the door at the end of our long hut, but I ignored it. I wasn't in a mood to be sociable. But the knocking went on. Finally I got up and went to open it. It was John. "You're being called on the tannoy," he said.

At the office, the receptionist said, "Your cousin rang. You, Ian and John have all passed."

She hadn't told the fellows about me because she wanted to tell me personally! But it hadn't been a bad experience to think I'd failed, and to come to God with nothing to offer him.

I continued to fill in my application papers for Wycliffe, now including the BD, but there was one question on the paper that stopped me in my tracks. It was something like, "Which part of the world do you think that God is calling you to?" Should I put Brazil? I'd always had a special interest in Brazil, but was that God's call? I didn't know. And I came across a verse in the Psalms that says, "God chose our inheritance for us." So I left it for him to choose. "Which part of the world...?" I wrote, "I'm willing to go wherever I'm needed," and handed the papers in.

Later I heard how the committee decided which country I should go to. They were discussing the candidates and had almost decided to send me to India. Wycliffe was just beginning to work among some of the minority languages there, and it was much easier for British missionaries to get visas than for Americans, so that seemed the obvious place for me. Until one of the committee members said, "This seems really silly. I've never even spoken to Joan, but as we're talking about her, I just have the feeling that God wants her in Brazil." He was a respected member of the committee and what he said carried weight. I was allocated to Brazil.

When we were all talking about it later that day, one of our staff members, a Wycliffe missionary working in Africa, said, "I hear you're going to Brazil. Lucky Brazil!" I was grateful that she thought well of me, but couldn't forget how useless I'd felt when I thought I'd failed my BD, and how God had accepted me even when I came to him with empty hands.

That was in the summer of 1965. There was the possibility, with certain provisos, of leaving England the next February to go to jungle training camp in Mexico on my way to Brazil. So what had to happen in the meantime? I needed finances – I had to raise a certain amount of money to cover my fare and my time in jungle camp. For the next few months, my job was to travel around the country visiting individuals and churches and talking about the work of Bible translation. Some of those people might be interested enough to help me financially, either then or in future years. And if they said, "Keep in touch," I was to take their details and add them to the list of people to whom I'd send a regular prayer letter when I was overseas. I'd need their prayers. And I'd need money too.

In Wycliffe we didn't get a salary. Every month, money that had been sent to the office for us would be forwarded on. And whatever unallocated money had come to the office would be shared out among those who needed it. We depended very much on the ongoing support of people who believed in what we were doing and wanted to have a part in it. But in truth, we depended on God. We believed that if we were doing what he wanted, he would make sure that we had what we needed. For that reason, I never felt comfortable asking for money. It was up to God to put the thought in people's minds. And he did. One time, when I was applying for a visa to go to Brazil, I was called into the office of the Brazilian Ambassador. He wanted to tell me that the amount of money that I'd be receiving was an extremely low wage! I assured him that it was fine – I knew I could manage on very little!

If I was to go in mid-February, there was a date a few weeks before when I had to have reached my target amount and could let the mission office know that I was ready to go. The day before that date I was in the Manchester area staying with my sister (by now she too had left Exclusive Brethren). I was about £50 short of my target, but I was going to tea with a wealthy family of former Exclusive Brethren whom we'd known for many years. They asked loads of questions about what my life was going to be like – it was all a new world to them – and they were quite fascinated and asked me to keep in touch. Our horizons as Brethren had been very narrow, so I was thrilled that they were feeling positive about something so strange and new to them. When I left, they gave me an envelope with a gift, probably the first they had ever given to overseas missions. As soon as I was on the bus going back to my sister's, I opened the envelope. Inside was £5. Of course, £5 then was considerably more in value than it is nowadays... But it wasn't the £50 that I needed. That was it. I couldn't leave in February.

Or could I? Back at Hilary's I had a bit of a strop. I said that it seemed really unfair. I'd done what I thought God wanted me to do. I'd worked hard at my part. But it didn't look as if God had done his part. (In subsequent years, I discovered that this is never true. If he does keep us waiting, there is always a good reason for it.) Later I rang my parents. To save me an expensive long-distance phone call the next day, I asked Mum to phone the Wycliffe office and tell them I hadn't quite raised the money I needed. But Mum had something to say to me. "There's a letter here for you from Birmingham," she said. "Do you want me to open it?" Of course I did! The envelope was from my church in Quinton with a letter saying that they'd been planning to give me some money at my farewell meeting, but thought perhaps it would be better to send it now. And there was a cheque for £50! God hadn't got his sums wrong!

Green lights all the way. All I needed now was to buy the required equipment, pack up, say my final goodbyes and go. Back in Essex, staying with my parents, we went shopping for things like an ex-army duffle bag for me to pack all the things I needed for jungle camp and a large metal drum to be shipped to Brazil with all the things I'd want there. I made appointments with the doctor for injections against tropical diseases. We bought an initial supply of malaria prophylaxis. My dad bravely went to the chemist to collect a five-year supply of sanitary protection that I'd ordered! The bedroom became full of clothing, books, photos, sleeping bag, jungle hammock... We had heard from the Brazil branch of Wycliffe what sort of things were not easily available there, and I was stocking up accordingly, preparing to be out of England for five years.

There was a farewell service at Westminster Chapel in London for about a dozen of us who were going to different parts of the world to work with Wycliffe. Six of us were heading for Brazil: Glyn and Cynthia Griffiths, Jim and Jenny Wilson with their baby Robert, and me. I was twenty-nine, still very single, but surrounded by loving family and friends. Several former Brethren came to that meeting in Westminster Chapel – one of them a friend of my dad, a man who had only recently left and had never been to anything like this in his whole life. I went up to him and Dad rather nervously at the end of the service. I thought he might be feeling a bit shocked by such things as lively music, women speaking in the service, women praying without hats, and so on. We ex-Exclusives were very shockable! But no, he was thrilled. "I felt the presence of Jesus here," he said.

There was also a smaller farewell service at my church in Quinton, Birmingham. It was an emotional experience saying goodbye and having so many people promise to pray for me during the years that I'd be away. Some fellow students from BBI were there, including Philip

Kearney and his wife Ann, who had come over on a motorbike from Leicester where they were now living. Such faithful friends!

All too soon the day of departure arrived. My kitbag for Mexico was all ready. The metal barrel for Brazil was not! My long-suffering dad and mum were going to pack that when I'd left and send it on its way to Brazil. They took me from Essex to the airport, where I'd arranged to meet Glyn and Cynthia for an overnight flight to New York via Reykjavik in Iceland. That was the cheapest way to cross the Atlantic in those days. Jim, Jenny and baby Robert had already gone to the States to visit relatives before going on to Mexico. There was quite a little crowd at the airport to see us off, with their friends and family and mine. Last hugs, a tear or two, and we were gone.

CHAPTER NINE

Jungle Camp in Mexico

1966

I don't remember much about the actual journey, except looking at a shop of Icelandic crafts at Reykjavik airport and feeling too sleepy to be very interested, and then arriving in New York. We had decided that in the few hours we had to wait for our flight to Mexico, we'd go into the city and see something interesting. But it was still a bit early for that, so I was prowling round the airport looking for some comfy seat to rest on and perhaps nod off for a few minutes after travelling all night. To my delight, I saw a door with the sign "Women's Rest Room". But it wasn't full of easy chairs as I'd imagined. It was all gleaming white tiles and cubicle doors – my first step in adjusting from British English to American English! After an hour or two, Glyn, Cynthia and I took a taxi into the city. We told the driver we had a few hours to spare and asked what he recommended we see. He took us to Macy's department store! Personally, I don't get excited about shopping, but there was one thing that Glyn was very interested to see – they were beginning to sell colour televisions!

Then on we travelled to Mexico City. There were Wycliffe people to meet us there and to take us to the Wycliffe headquarters, where we were to stay for a few days. There we'd meet people who were working in Mexico fulltime and others, like ourselves, who were in the country for a few months of training in how to live in a remote jungle situation.

At the evening meal one day I sat with an American family who were in Mexico long-term, and I experienced another culture clash. One young lad was using his knife and fork as we do in the UK, possibly copying this strange English woman who was sharing their table, but his mother corrected him. "Don't hold your knife and fork like that. You look like a farmer. Use your knife to cut your meat, then put your knife down and eat with your fork in your right hand." Oops! I was too shy to laugh and say he was probably copying me. At that time I would still go quiet and feel uncomfortable when I was with people I didn't know well. It would have been so much better to laugh and explain.

A couple of days later we travelled down to Chiapas in the south of Mexico to begin our stay in jungle camp. The last part of the journey was by a small four-seater plane. All the passengers and their baggage had to be weighed to keep each flight down to a safe weight. I apologised to the missionary-pilot that I was heavier than some of the other women. "Oh, don't worry," he said. "In the last group for jungle camp, there was a girl so heavy I had to warn her that if she put on any more weight, I'd have to fly her out in two loads!"

For the first six weeks we were at main base, where there were wooden buildings for us to sleep in, a kitchen where we took turns helping with the cooking and a dining-room-cum-lecture-room. Lectures? Not again! But this time they were about very practical subjects like anthropology, survival and health – our own, and giving medical help to others when in a situation far from doctors and hospitals. In the afternoons, we went off on hikes and canoe trips. Once we went to visit a village of the Lacandon tribe. We women were warned not to go into their god-house – it was strictly for the men – but we were allowed to look in through the doorway. There was a shelf there with a row of clay vases on it. These were the "god pots", each one reputedly containing a spirit god who was to be worshipped and feared. The atmosphere in the village was very sad and forbidding. I felt so thankful that my God isn't a dark, frightening being living in a clay pot on a shelf.

Because the river running past main base was fairly shallow, to propel the canoe along it was necessary to use a pole, a bit like the students at Cambridge punting on the Cam. To do this, of course, you have to stand, and it's easy to feel insecure and overbalance. One afternoon I was in a canoe with Jim and an outdoorsy American from

Oregon. Had I had my eyes shut going through a rapid? Perhaps so, because I'd missed the moment when they must have hatched a plot together. The first thing I knew was that the canoe began rocking madly from side to side, and the second was that I'd been tipped into the water! I came up spluttering to see the two men standing in a now perfectly stable boat, roaring with laughter! Actually, though, they did me a favour. I'd fallen in the river once and come to no harm – there was no point in being nervous any more. One of my most fun memories of jungle camp was when we went downstream one afternoon, camped out by the river overnight, and raced back upstream in the morning, poling through the smooth water and dragging the boat up through the rapids.

The survival training culminated in a survival hike. All the women were taken out of jungle camp one day and led through the forest to an area where we'd never been before. There we had to scatter, each to a place at least a hundred yards from anyone else, and build ourselves a shelter made of branches and leaves, where we could take cover for the night. We were to imagine ourselves the only survivor of a plane crash, so were not allowed to communicate with each other. We had known that a survival hike was going to happen soon, so for a day or two had been carrying matches in our pockets, along with toilet paper and anything else we thought essential. Once our shelter was built, we were able to light a little fire to keep any wild animals at bay, and to settle down as the night began. I had a small New Testament with me, and as I opened it to read a verse or two before it got dark, out fell a little card that my grandmother had given me. "He who watches over Israel will neither slumber nor sleep." How appropriate! Actually, I didn't do much slumbering myself either. I had to put more wood on the fire to keep it going until morning. And during the night it started to rain, and I wished I'd put a few more branches on my roof. It's not easy to sleep when drips of rain are running down your neck! Because of the rain, a nearby tree was uprooted and fell with a great crashing of branches. I did break the rules then, and yelled across to a friend that I knew was in that direction, "You all right?"

"Yes, fine thanks." That was enough.

When the dawn comes and you know it's morning, it's strange not to have anything for breakfast except a few gulps of water from a metal water bottle – it makes you appreciate the normal blessings of life!

When the men had their survival hike, one group went off to a new area and were to camp out there until the others found them and brought them safely back. They had supplies for two days, but there was some mistake about the area they had gone to, and in the event, they were there for five days and their supplies ran out. They decided that the others were never going to find them and they might as well make their own way back. Good lessons learned in case we ever were in a real survival situation.

For the second half of jungle camp, we moved to advance base. Here, each married couple and each twosome of single people had to build our own "champa", or little hut, with the help of a local tribesman. I shared with Muriel, a slim little lady who was going to stay in Mexico. Our helper had been busy making our "furniture"; we came back to find one small bed for Muriel, and something more like a dining table. This, we discovered, was my bed! Made to measure! The beds couldn't be moved because they were made by knocking four posts into the ground for the corners, then putting a layer of slats across a frame to make a base for the sleeping bags, so my outsize bed dominated our little champa for the whole time we were there! We now lived more independently than at main base and cooked for ourselves on a fire in our own champas.

One Sunday evening we gathered round a campfire and each told our story of where we'd come from and where we were going. One girl from an American city said that she had never walked farther than a block in her life – she would always get the car out or go by cab. Our strenuous life at jungle camp must have been quite a shock for her. That was a wonderful evening – so inspiring to realise what a mixture of different people we were, but each with a readiness to embark on a whole new way of life in a totally alien environment. And here we were, together in one place for just a few short weeks. I was extremely impressed with one young American on his way to West Africa. He explained how he wanted to adapt totally to living as the people he would be working among did – to dress as they did, eat as they did, talk as they did, think as they did. "That really is making a great sacrifice, just as Jesus did in becoming a human being to get close to us," I thought. Sadly, a few years later, I heard that the stress had been too much for this keen young American; he'd had a breakdown and been forced to return to the States. What a disappointing end to a very brave experiment.

Once when we were on a long hike, I stupidly repeated the same mistake I'd made at the airport in New York. After some hours' walking, our leader announced that it was a "rest stop". Grateful for a break, I sat down on the grass under the trees. The other women all went off in one direction, but I stayed where I was to rest. It was some minutes before I realised that a rest stop isn't just to rest, in the same way that the rest room at the airport existed for quite another purpose!

Over the years in South America, where most of my colleagues were from North America, I had to learn many words of new vocabulary. I've since heard it described as "two countries divided by a common language"! A tap is a "faucet", a jug is a "pitcher", a mum is a "mom", post is "mail", a biscuit is a "cookie", a scone is a "biscuit", and so on. And it's not just words, it's attitudes as well. I was shocked that an American friend always bought two of everything, one to use now and one to have in hand. "How wasteful!" I thought. But then it dawned on me that if I'm thinking, "How wasteful!" my American friend is probably looking at me and thinking, "How stingy!" It's all a question of what we're used to.

It was relaxing to spend time with other people from the UK, with whom we didn't have to adjust our vocabulary, or adapt our behaviour. Jim worked out a way for Jenny to bake a cake on the wood fire, and I was invited to their champa one Sunday for a very British afternoon tea. Such a treat! And little Robert was a delight. The central storeroom bought supplies of eggs or fruit from local people, and when there was enough to share out, a shout of "bodega" would be passed along from champa to champa. "Bodega" is the Spanish for a warehouse of supplies. When we heard it, we'd all go along to the centre of the camp to collect our share of the goodies. That was one of Robert's first words. He'd join in and shout "bodega" too.

When the time came to leave jungle camp and return to Mexico City, we were put into teams to build rafts and then pole them downstream to the airstrip. Getting back into the city was entering a strangely different world. The pavements were hard under our feet. The glass shop windows were incredibly big and shiny. The people were unbelievably well dressed. We felt scruffy, out of place, and desperately in need of a hot bath and a visit to the hairdresser! But what a fabulous three months we'd had. We could hardly wait to get to a tribal situation of our own.

Learning how to canoe.

CHAPTER TEN

Brasília

1966 - 1967

For me, getting to the tribes was still quite a time away. We eventually got to Brazil, but there could be no going off to the backwoods until we'd spent time in town learning Portuguese and becoming a bit more used to finding our way around. Brasília was a very new capital city at that time with a great deal of construction work still in progress. It was going to be very grand, built with splendid buildings, wide roads and attractive apartment blocks behind well-kept green lawns. Because it is on the central plateau of Brazil, the land is fairly flat and that means there is always a wide expanse of sky, a feeling of space. Even in hot weather you feel you can breathe in Brasília. In wet weather, there were sometimes problems. Before the city was built, rainfall was measured and careful calculations were made to ensure that the drainage system would be adequate to cope with any tropical downpour. Then a dam was built, a river valley was flooded to form a lake and, unexpectedly, a microclimate developed with a much heavier rainfall than was expected. I once walked back through waist-deep floods to the place where I was living, but that's not a major problem in a hot country where it's easy to dry off afterwards. It was said that most of the people in government still lived in Rio de Janeiro, flew up to Brasília for important meetings, but rushed back to the comforts of a more established city whenever they could. But those weren't the circles that we expected to move in!

After a short time in the mission house near the newly-built Brasília, we moved out to live with Brazilian families in one of the satellite towns a few miles away. It was called Taguatinga and was very different from the main new, carefully planned area. It had grown up to house people working in the new capital, and many commuted in daily in crowded, rickety buses. The streets of Taguatinga were not tarred, and the houses varied from nice little bungalows to makeshift shacks. But there were shops and churches and quite a thriving community.

The house where I lodged was a bungalow made of concrete blocks, owned by a pleasant young couple from one of the local Protestant churches, so I went to church with them and got to know some of their friends. When I was first there, my Portuguese was extremely limited, and I was capable of causing much embarrassment and amusement. One story that went all round the neighbourhood related to a birthday cake for the little son of my host family. I had discovered that if I didn't know the Portuguese word I needed, it was sometimes possible to use a French word and give it a Portuguese accent. The languages are somewhat similar and some words are almost exactly the same. So when I came into the house one day and saw my hostess icing a birthday cake, I adapted the French word "gateau" for cake, and came out with "O que gato lindo!" hoping that I was saying, "Oh, what a beautiful cake!" but found that I'd actually said, "Oh, what a beautiful cat!" They didn't let me forget that one! They also got a lot of amusement from the fact that I used their little boy's books as practice for reading Portuguese. Large print, limited vocabulary, short sentences – it was ideal for a beginner. But the family were vastly amused to hear this foreign woman earnestly following the adventures of a naughty puppy dog! Do you remember me as a younger woman, scared of making a mistake when I was trying to speak French? Something seemed to be changing at last.

Our Portuguese course was supposed to last for six months, but the mission asked if I'd be willing to be pulled out after only about three months. Wycliffe had an agreement with the American School in Brasília that we would provide a teacher whose salary would be used to help mission families to pay the school fees for their children. The teacher who was due to come down from the States that term was ill. Would I be willing to take her place for a few months? I was disappointed, both because it meant not completing the Portuguese course, and because it might delay my going to work with a tribe in the Amazon forest. But I could see that it was better for Wycliffe to use me for the job than to have to interrupt someone else's programme, so I agreed to go back to teaching for a while.

The American School was held in a rather luxurious apartment block in the new city of Brasília, so I left Taguatinga and, in order to keep on practising Portuguese, moved to stay with the widow of a Brazilian brigadier and her two grown-up daughters in another apartment in the city. They were very kind and I learned a lot from them about Brazilian attitudes. One day the "senhora" told me that I walked just like an American, with my elbows held back and my head held high – a Brazilian lady would have her shoulders more relaxed and would look a lot more feminine! Also a Brazilian lady would not go out alone – I was much too independent! The younger daughter of the family, perhaps in her early twenties, was invited to spend a Saturday going to a swimming pool with an eligible young man, and I was asked to go along as her chaperone. It was a new role that I'd not experienced before, but I took a book and hoped I was maintaining her good name without being too intrusive. During the afternoon, the eligible gentleman asked me to move and sit somewhere away from them. I checked that it was what she wanted too, and went to the opposite side of the swimming pool, but I was slightly anxious that they might leave without me and I'd be left without a lift back to the city. What a strange, bewildering thing it is to be living in a different country with limited language and minimal awareness of the niceties of etiquette!

One day I did make a major mistake. It was Good Friday and I was not at school. My room was in a bit of a mess and I asked the live-in maid for a brush to sweep the bedroom floor. The senhora said nothing to me, but I heard her rebuking the girl. "It's a holy day. You know very well that you don't get the brushes out!" Oh dear, failed again! And this time the little maid was blamed for my mistake.

In Brasília, I attended a Pentecostal church where the part-time pastor was a high-ranking soldier in the Brazilian army. One Sunday he told us an amazing story. In the course of his duties that week, he had been driven to Goiânia for an important military conference. As he was leaving, some soldiers were forming a guard of honour from the doorway of the building to the car where his chauffeur was waiting. He had passed them and was about to get into the car, when he knew that

God was speaking to him. God told him that one of the young soldiers he had just walked by was actually planning to murder someone. For a moment he hesitated – it didn't seem appropriate to turn back and speak to one of the guard of honour. But no, God had spoken and he had to do something about it. He turned back and told the man what God had said to him. "I beg of you, don't do it. Don't ruin your life. God loves you and has told me to warn you." The young soldier coloured deeply and turned away. The pastor-cum-general got in the car and left. He told us the story as an encouragement to each of us to keep our ears open to God, and to be unafraid to pass on God's messages to the people we meet.

This was my living situation in Brasília, but what about work? How was I getting on in the American School? I had a class of eight-year-old children and quite a detailed syllabus to follow. That was a help – I didn't have to wonder what I was supposed to teach them. Some things were rather different from in England. I remember being amused that I was teaching the American War of Independence from the point of view that the British were the enemy! There was one English child in the class – her father worked in the British Embassy – and I quietly said to her that we were looking at the story from the American point of view. I didn't want her to think I was being unpatriotic.

There was sometimes a little difficulty in that the children of Wycliffe missionaries knew me as "Aunt Joan" out of school. One, a girl called Cindy, decided to take advantage of that relationship and not co-operate in school. Each Friday we had a spelling test on the words they had learned that week, and each Friday, as we were about to begin the test, Cindy would be unable to find her pencil. At first I waited patiently while she rummaged in her desk. After a week or two, I began the test anyway and gave her the first word while everyone else was on number three. Then one week, I told the class to get out their pencils for the spelling test and said to Cindy that I was going to say each word only twice and, if she missed it, there wouldn't be another opportunity. She still didn't have her pencil ready, but I ignored her and went through the test. By the end, she had got herself organised and got the last three correct; so I put her mark of 3 in my book when everyone else had got 9 or 10. I don't know what she said to her parents, but they knew that she had got a 3 out of 10 in my mark book. At our next meeting of Wycliffe members in the city, her mother came to have a quiet word with me, very distressed, afraid it would affect Cindy's grades at the end of term. I asked her not to tell Cindy – she needed to learn her lesson – but I reassured the mother that the mark in my book was in brackets, and wouldn't affect Cindy's end-of-term grade. After that, I had an uncomfortable feeling that Cindy's parents didn't like me very much, but I had a job to do and couldn't let mission children be favoured over embassy children.

I had gone to Brazil expecting to work in the forest, and it was sometimes a sartorial challenge that I was now in the city, involved in the American School, and mixing with people from the diplomatic services, going to the occasional cocktail party, and meeting visiting American senators, as well as an astronaut. I hadn't the wardrobe for that sort of thing and, to be honest, hadn't the experience either, but the headmaster required all his staff to be there for such functions. I may have looked out of place, but inwardly I often raised a quizzical eyebrow at the situations I found myself in. At one cocktail party, I was trapped for a time at the side of a table by two young men from the embassy who were "talking to impress", about something I knew absolutely nothing about. I whiled away the time munching crisps and cheese, and made my getaway as soon as I could squeeze past. Later that same evening, the visiting senator, now rather tipsy, invited me to go back to his hotel, but I was able to make my excuses and say I had already arranged to go home with friends. The prim young sister from England, dressed in her simple homemade dress, was certainly out of her element here! I didn't have the money to buy a lavish new dress, and even if I had, it would have been a total waste of money – it would have spent the rest of its life in a suitcase while I went off to the forest.

How was the money situation? Were those gifts from the UK adequate for life in the city? Well, amazingly, there was always enough. Just before Christmas that year, my neck and cheeks swelled up as if I had mumps, and I had to go and see the doctor. He diagnosed it as an infection from some tropical sores in my hair, gave me antibiotics and, as I was leaving, came to the door to shake me by the hand. I thought he was being very courteous, but realised later that his outstretched hand was more likely a reminder that I owed him some money for the consultation. Our British NHS had not prepared me for this! I went back later and discovered that there was a bill of about £80 to be paid. The next time my allowance came from the UK, it included a letter from a group of ex-Brethren who explained that they had been praying for me and, at the end of the meeting, had had a whip-round to send me a gift. The amount they had collected was about £80. This must have happened weeks before my medical bill, but God's timing had been spot on as usual!

At the end of my time at the school, I received a cheque from the headmaster for several thousand dollars, which I was delighted to hand in at our Wycliffe office as a contribution to the children's school fees. It was a great moment to have thousands of dollars to give to the mission. And in spite of my initial negative feelings, I was glad that my first year in Brazil had worked out that way. Doing a familiar job and having a roomful of youngsters to love had been a great help in leaving family and my home country and moving out into the unknown. I felt that God had been very kind to me.

I was free to go to a tribe at last but the question was, which tribe and where? Do you remember Sheila Tremaine, who had come to Birmingham Bible Institute to tell us about the Rikbaktsa tribe and the gnat-filled part of the forest where they lived? I'd been so glad that Sheila and her colleague Valerie were already covering that situation. But around the time I was completing my responsibilities at the school in Brasília, Valerie, after repeated attacks of severe malaria, had been told that she should not return to that area, but should move to a tribal situation where malaria was not so prevalent. Sheila was looking for a new colleague to work with her. Would I go?

Brasília.

CHAPTER ELEVEN

Life with the Rikbaktsa

1967 - 1975

I agreed to work with Sheila and the Rikbaktsa tribe, and moved on from Brasília to Cuiabá, the capital of the state of Mato Grosso. One blessing of being in Cuiabá was that my friends Glyn and Cynthia were also based there and returned periodically from their tribe many miles to the south. Jim and Jenny were there too, running a children's home for Wycliffe children whose parents were working in remote tribes. More than once when I came back to town from the tribe in future years, I stayed in that house with Jim and Jenny. A comfortable bed, a pile of magazines from England, and friends to talk to – what more could I ask?

My immediate job was to make preparations for my first session in a tribal village. I needed jeans and long-sleeved blouses as protection against the gnats, supplies of batteries for my torch and tape-recorder, paper to write letters and to record phonetically whatever words I could pick up, books for study and relaxation, vitamin pills to make up for a lack of fruit and vegetables, and whatever food we would need for a stay of some months. Fortunately for me, Sheila was well used to all this and could help me get myself ready. This was also a good time to send out a prayer letter to friends and supporters in the UK. There was not going to be a postbox in the tribal village!

We travelled first by truck for a couple of days from Cuiabá to a settlement on the River Juruena called Porto dos Gauchos (meaning

"Cowboys' Port"). This was the end of the roads at that time. At the settlement, trees had been felled and a little township was growing up with people making a living from cattle farming, trading and collecting rubber. The rubber trees were not in a plantation, but growing naturally, dotted around in the forest. The rubber tappers lived in isolated houses along the riverside and would walk miles through the forest visiting the rubber trees and collecting the sap. Every few weeks a motorboat came down the river from the settlement to bring in some supplies for the rubber tappers and their families and take out the now-solidified blocks of raw rubber. That boat was our transport from Porto dos Gauchos to our Rikbaktsa village, about five days' journey away. By day we sat in the boat delighting in the jungle scenery – the macaws, the monkeys, the clouds of butterflies. Very occasionally, we'd see a big cat, perhaps an ocelot, sunning itself on a rock by the river. At night we might hang our hammocks in the house of a rubber tapper, if there was space, or the boatmen might make a fire to cook some rice for our supper and we'd just put our hammocks under the trees.

The first night of my first journey downriver, we hung our hammocks in the house of a rubber tapper. He lived there, year in year out, with his wife, and they had recently been joined by a young woman on her own. My hammock was next to hers and, as we settled down for the night, she told me her story. She had been living some miles away with her common-law husband, but their peace was shattered when a lone man who was mentally unstable appeared out of the forest one day. He had a gun and he shot and killed her husband.

"Whatever did you do?" I asked.

To which she replied, "I took the gun and shot him, buried them both, and came down to live here. I didn't fancy being on my own."

It was her being so matter-of-fact about it that shook me – her treating evil and tragedy as if they were the norm. These were Portuguese-speaking Brazilians, not tribespeople. As time went on, I came to realise that quite a proportion of these forest dwellers were there because they needed to get away from the law. As they told us, "No policeman would dare to come down our river." Remarkably, we were kept safe and usually unafraid. We used the phrase "going out" to describe leaving the forest for a few weeks in Cuiabá, and "coming in" for returning to the tribe, so the Bible verse, "The Lord will watch over your going out and coming in from this time forth and for evermore," was a promise of deep significance to us.

Our mail was transported in the same way. Letters would arrive for us in Cuiabá and be collected by a representative of the mission. From time to time he'd contact the office of the rubber firm and find out when the next boat was going downriver to send us our large packet of mail. We had radio contact about once a week with our mission base in Cuiabá and they'd let us know roughly when the boat was coming so that we could have ready whatever letters we needed to send out. When a pack of letters arrived, we gave ourselves a holiday and spent some time reading and enjoying all the news. One time, when some of the tribesmen came to our house, they were puzzled about why this bundle of paper was so important and interesting. I tried to think of something I'd read that would make any sense at all to them, and came up with the fact that my parents were moving to a different house. The men were very concerned. "When you go back to your old clearing," they said, "will there be someone there to show you the way to your parents' new clearing?" It was a totally different worldview from ours, but I was moved to see their concern that I might have lost touch with my parents forever. Human kindness transcends all cultural differences.

In that first journey along the river, in the last few miles of travel, one of the crew of the boat said to me, "There are your people!" – and there, paddling a canoe near the bank of the river, were three Rikbaktsa men. The motorboat pulled over to them and the Brazilians invited them to tie their canoe behind the boat and come aboard. It was all very quiet. Nobody spoke to me. But for me it was high drama.

These were indeed to be "my people" for a few years, and I was noticing all I could about them. I saw their straight black hair, left to grow long at the back but cut in a fringe across their foreheads. I saw their earlobes pierced so that a round disc of balsa wood could be put in the hole. The discs of the younger men were small, but it looked as if the earlobe must expand over the years because an older man had quite a large disc. I saw how they spoke to one another and listened without looking at one another. "That's going to make language learning hard," I thought, "if I'm not supposed to look at the person who's talking to me."

And it certainly wasn't easy. The Rikbaktsa spoke very quietly. Those in our village knew only their own language, a "monolingual situation" we called it, so it was not possible to ask them a question in Portuguese or any other language. We just had to observe and listen and try to discover how they ask questions, in what situations they use which words, and so on. Sheila told me how she and Valerie had first been able to make a tiny start in the language. They'd been down to the river one day – the village was actually by a stream a short walk up from the Juruena river – and, as they were walking back to the house, they met someone carrying an empty water pot who said to them "Pihikbo my." Could that mean, "I'm going for water"? Sheila got to the house, picked up a bucket and set off back to the river saying to everyone she met, "Pihikbo my." And they all smiled and looked pleased, as if to say, "These crazy foreigners are not totally dumb after all!"

Later came similar phrases, such as, "Wahorobo my," for when they are going back to their house, and thus the vocabulary grew. Sheila now had:

pihik	*water, river*
wahoro	*house*
-bo	*to, for*
my	*I (am going)*

Slowly and painstakingly our list of words and our understanding of how they fit together in this particular language increased. It was going to be a long, long time before we could begin to translate the Bible but bit by bit, with God's help, we hoped to get there.

The "wahoro" that Sheila and I lived in was very like the houses in the rest of the village. Its floor was well-trodden earth. Its walls were made of strong corner-posts – tree trunks knocked into the ground – walls of mud-covered branches between the corner posts. Its roof was layers of folded palm fronds. One difference in our house was that the upper part of the walls was mosquito netting to let in some light so that we could see to read. The Rikbaktsa preferred their houses to be dark to discourage the gnats. Another difference was that our door was made of planks that had been brought in for the purpose. Their doors were usually just palm fronds fastened together.

Because of the all the insects, it was extremely bad manners to hover in someone's doorway. One had to leap in quickly and pull the palm fronds across, or there would be angry little shouts of "Hokbo ty!" which is literally, "To the hole imperative!" meaning, "Shut the door!"

Traditional clothing for the Rikbaktsa people had been an apron of shredded tree bark for the men, and just long rows and rows of seed necklaces for the women. But that left a lot of uncovered skin for the gnats to attack, and the people were eager to wear more clothing. By the time I went there, the men had cotton shorts or trousers, sometimes with a shirt, and most women had a cotton dress. They liked us to trade clothing or fabric with them for the meat they brought back from hunting or the fish they caught in the river. We also "paid" them in useful goods for the hours they spent teaching us their language, but it was not always easy to find something they wanted. One man, Tawamy, came most evenings and spent an hour working with Sheila, talking into the tape recorder and trying to explain the meaning of something in a way she would understand. After a while, she offered him a new hammock in payment. He wouldn't accept it, and seemed nonplussed by the offer. Why would he need a hammock when he already had one? Perhaps a couple of fishhooks? Money did not exist for them, our money values were irrelevant, and the concept of wanting more possessions than one's neighbour was totally ludicrous. We could only stand back in amazed admiration.

There were other things about the Rikbaktsa that made us feel as though our civilisation was morally inferior to theirs. It was a puzzle to them that we were both unmarried. One time when they asked us again why we were single, Sheila said that there had been a war where we lived and a lot of the men had been killed. It was a slight anachronism since we had both been young children at the time of the Second World War, but it was an explanation that had some meaning for them.

They wanted some more details and, holding up five fingers, asked, "Were this many killed?"

"It was more."

They were shocked and held up both hands. "Was it this many?"

"It was more."

No way could we begin to describe a war that had killed thousands upon thousands. It was beyond their numerical understanding, but more significantly, we were too ashamed. In Portuguese, the word for the people of the tribes is "indígenos" or "índios" (indigenous people or

Indians), and for the rest of society "civilizados" (civilised ones). This conversation about war made me wonder who are truly more civilised.

Following logically along this line of thinking brought me to the question of why I'd come to be a missionary to them. What did I have to give them? How could I truly enrich them? Civilising them was not part of it. There were things about their attitudes to admire; there were also things to deplore. But I could say exactly the same about the attitudes of Western civilisation. Education, medicine – yes, perhaps those things could help them somewhat, especially as their hidden forest world was soon to be invaded by the roads and commercial interests of encroaching development. But the one vitally important thing I would love to share with them was the knowledge of God. I saw their fear of going to the river after dark, because of the evil spirit who lives in the rapids and can suck them into the water, and I felt so thankful to know a God who "watches over" me. I saw their desperate, exhausting dancing hour after hour to appease the god of the harvest and ensure a harvest the next year, and I praised the God who makes sure I am not in want. If only they could know him too.

The first few months in the tribe were not an easy time. Having a new colleague was not great for Sheila. Valerie had been very domesticated, a good homemaker and an excellent cook. Those are not my skills! I needed reminding to tidy the house and sweep the floor when visitors had dropped banana skins everywhere. I could light the fire and cook our rice and fish, but it wasn't guaranteed to taste delicious! No, it wasn't a great exchange from Sheila's point of view. And then, in the evening, when it was dark and the local people had gone to their hammocks, I wasn't good at relaxing and being sociable. I was more likely to be reading by the light of our paraffin lamp, looking something up in a linguistics textbook, trying to refresh my memory after long months away from linguistics in jungle camp and at the American School.

It wasn't the easiest time for me either. I still used to feel quite shy sometimes. Going into the homes of the local people, listening to their conversation without invitation, scribbling down in phonetics what I thought I'd heard – all this made me feel as if I was intruding into their lives. However, there was one woman who made me feel at home. When I went to her house, she would say, "Nabeti dyhyty!" (sit there) and show me a piece of tree trunk where I could perch out of everyone's way and watch and listen. One morning when I was sitting there, her husband came in from hunting. Slung on his back was a big black monkey that he had killed with his bow and arrows. She began to prepare it for cooking and, bless her, cut off an arm and gave it to me. Sheila wasn't impressed when I took it home. She said that the families who knew us well would be aware of the fact that we don't eat monkey meat. But I was really grateful. I felt I had a friend.

Very shortly afterwards, however, my friend had a bad attack of malaria and died. I was devastated. And, to be honest, I was furious. Back at home, in the house alone, I knelt on the earth floor and poured out my feelings. It must have been something like, "Oh God, I can't cope with this. You've brought me all this way and through all these years of training to tell her about you. And now you've let her die before I've begun to have any words to tell her. How could you do that?" I stayed there quite a while, churned up and miserable.

And then it was as if God said, "You think you care about her. But you've known her only a few weeks; I've known her since before she was born. You've hardly been able to communicate with her at all; I've known every thought she has thought, every feeling she has felt, throughout her entire life."

Until that time, without giving it a great deal of thought, I'd subscribed to the view of some evangelical Christians that in order to be saved for eternity, people need to know and accept that Jesus has died for them. Since that day, I've believed that because of the death of Jesus, God can save even people who don't know about it. Otherwise, what hope would there be for all the godly people who lived in the ages before Christ, for those with severe learning difficulties who cannot understand, or for a lady of the Rikbaktsa tribe who died a few years too soon? My sense of justice is not more highly developed than God's! "Shall not the Judge of all the earth do right?"

Child learning how to be a woman.

CHAPTER TWELVE

Medical Work in the Forest

1967 - 1975

Because there were no doctors or hospitals for hundreds of miles from our village, we always had some common medicines available, and would do whatever we could to help when people were ill. The most frequent illness was malaria, and in our region the malaria was "chloroquine resistant", which meant that, even taking regular prophylaxis, we were liable to get ill ourselves. Another recurrent illness for the local people was the common cold, but for them it was more serious than for us because it was a relatively recent virus for them and they hadn't built up the resistance to it that those from the UK have. In fact, when Father John from the Catholic Missão Anchieta had discovered this tribe about a generation before we were there, there had been a terrible epidemic of colds or influenza that had killed hundreds of Rikbaktsa people. By the time we were there, there were only about five hundred of the tribe left, scattered between our village, three villages where the Missão Anchieta still worked and a few very small groups living in remote, less-accessible places, far from the main river. We always made sure that we had plenty of tablets and injections for those diseases, plus some antibiotics and antibacterial lotions and ointments to try, and tried to be prepared for whatever else might come our way. At the Missão Anchieta, a couple of days journey away, there was a nun called Sister Salete who had medicines too, as well as some skill in dentistry.

Sometimes, when our patients seemed very ill or we were unsure if our treatment was what was really needed, we would also pray for them. At first our knowledge was too limited to pray in the vernacular, so we would pray in Portuguese, but tell them we were talking to Jesus about them. Some years later, when the villagers we knew moved to live on the reservation around where the Missão Anchieta was working, Sister Salete told us about something that had interested and challenged her. More than once when she was treating a patient who had come from our area, after they had downed their medicine they would hang about waiting. The first time, she tried to move them on. "That's okay now. You've had what you need today. Come back tomorrow morning."

Not to be daunted, they explained why they were waiting: "Aren't you going to talk to Him-up-there about me?"

If that was one way that we were a challenge to her, there were other ways in which Sister Salete challenged us. I was at her village one time and, seeing her walking around quietly on her own, went over and asked her a question. She smiled but didn't reply. The next day she was apologetic and explained that she had been having a quiet day when she did a lot of praying and thinking about God, but tried not to talk to anyone. I saw the importance of that and realised it would be a valuable practice in my own life. Salete was particularly enjoying discovering the Bible. For centuries it had been the custom for Catholics not to read the Bible individually, but to have it read and interpreted for them by the priest in church. Now Salete was reading it by herself and discovering treasures there that felt like God talking directly to her. Sometimes she would find a special verse and say to me, "Have you ever heard this before? I'd no idea that the Bible says this sort of thing." Usually I had heard the verse before, but I realised that my familiarity with it had robbed me of the excitement that she was feeling. Since then I have often tried to read the Bible in other languages or different translations, in order to experience something of the impact that she was feeling.

Thinking of medical matters reminds me of a time when Sheila was back in the UK caring for her father who was ill. One month there was a serious epidemic in our village. Without a handy laboratory to find out what the disease was, the only thing we knew was that it was not malaria, because it didn't respond to malaria medicine. But it was giving several people a high fever and making them very ill indeed. Two people had died – a young man and a little boy called Daví. Several others were seriously ill. I spent a long time late one afternoon going from house to house with my little box of medicines, doing what I could, praying inwardly, fighting against the spirit of fear and despair that was beginning to engulf the village. One mother begged me to give her baby more medicine, but I had already given him what I could to combat his pain and fever.

"My baby's going to be the next to die," she pleaded. "He won't be alive by the morning."

On the spur of the moment I replied, "No, your baby will get well. There's a man in the sky called Jesus. He will take care of your baby tonight."

I went out of her house thinking I'd been an utter fool. She was new to our village and had probably heard nothing before about Jesus. I could well have added to her fears by letting her think that this mysterious unseen man was looking at her child. The fear in the village was beginning to get to me too. The thought crossed my mind that if there had been a bus stop there, I'd have got on the bus and left my responsibilities in the village forever. But no bus stop, no way out.

I went back to our house. Staying with me for a while in Sheila's absence was a colleague who normally worked as a librarian in Brasília. She was ill with her first bout of malaria, and I'd left her sleeping a couple of hours before. Now, as I arrived back, she was rushing out of the house to find me, very afraid. She was usually a calm, quiet person, but not at that moment. She had been lying on a camp bed at the back of the house, and had heard the creak of our door. Over the palm-frond partition, she could see the top of the door as it opened, and imagined someone coming in – not a tall person, because she couldn't see anyone's head. Then, round the corner of the partition, came a little red figure, ugly and terrifying. She screamed the name of Jesus, it disappeared, and she was running to find me. We talked and prayed, helpless, but trusting that God would somehow find a way to bring peace to that troubled village. We had a meagre meal of a boiled egg and a slice of home-baked bread. Then we went to sleep.

The next morning, I woke early and heard people crying again in the ritual way that they mourned a death. I went out of the house to a lovely sunny dawn, but with returning grief in my heart. My friend Red Macaw was going past on his way to the river.

"Who has died in the night?" I asked him.

"Nobody."

"Then why are the people crying?"

"Oh, it's just that they didn't cry enough yesterday for Daví. Nobody else is going to die now."

I looked puzzled. How could he be so sure?

"Didn't you hear the rain in the night?" he explained. "When it rains, the ducks get very busy and they eat up all the evil spirits."

I hadn't heard that before! But it was a new day, the sun was shining, the fear was gone. God had known how to bring calm and comfort to a grieving village.

After a quick breakfast, I went round to the home of the lady who thought that her baby was going to be the next to die. How would he be? He was sleeping peacefully at his mother's breast. "Him-up-there," she said with a smile, "he didn't go to sleep last night, did he?"

So far, when I had prayed with them, I had prayed in Portuguese. It's not easy to pray in a language that you are only just learning, especially if you've never heard any other prayer in that language. I remember the first time I tried. The men had been out hunting, and a young lad called Dopy had gone with them for the first time. He must have been about ten years old. He was doing very well keeping up with the men as they ran along the narrow jungle trails. They came to a place where there was a rotting log across the path. The men were able to take it in their stride and jump over it, but Dopy, with shorter legs, stepped on top of the log. The wood crumbled under his weight, and a scorpion hiding in the log stung him on the foot.

They carried him back to the village, but he was in extreme pain. A scorpion sting has a poison that affects the entire nervous system. In the smaller body of a child it can be fatal. The men arrived back just as it was getting dark, and Dopy's father came round to our house to tell us what had happened. I understand that there is an anti-venin to counteract scorpion stings, but it needs to be kept refrigerated, so there was no possibility for us to keep a supply in a place without electricity. We could do nothing medically to help. But we went round to their house and sat there watching Dopy writhing in his hammock in pain.

After a while I could stand it no longer. I told them I was going to talk to Jesus about Dopy, and I prayed in their language. It must have been the simplest of prayers. Perhaps something like, "Because of the scorpion, Dopy is hurting a lot. We cannot do anything. But, Jesus, you know everything. Take the pain away and make him better." There isn't a word for "please" in the language, and I didn't know how to show respect. It just had to be a bald request. And Dopy continued to writhe and groan.

I moved to sit away from the fire in the dark shadows at the back of the house. And now I was praying silently, desperately. "I'm so sorry if I've got it wrong. I'm so sorry if you didn't want me to pray for his healing. But I've done it now. And if you don't make Dopy better, they'll think you can't do it. Oh God, please, please don't let them think that you're powerless." Tears on my face, I went back to join the circle.

Suddenly Dopy stopped groaning and sat up. "Can I have a drink of water?" he asked. His mother gave him a gourd of water; he drank it and said, "I'm going to sleep now," and lay still and peaceful in his hammock.

The next morning, his father was at our door. "Are you going to say thank you to Jesus?" he said. "I want to hear you say thank you."

One time when Sheila was away, I was invited by the priest of the Missão Anchieta, Padre Edgar, to go and work in one of their villages. I accepted gladly, grateful to have the opportunity to continue my language learning without the isolation of living in our more distant village. As we were going along the river in the motorboat, I must have been rather quiet.

"Are you all right?" said the priest. "I can turn round and take you back if you want."

"No, I'm fine. I'm looking forward to being back in the tribe."

"That's okay then," he said in a fatherly way, "but everyone has their limit. Don't be embarrassed to say if this is all too much for you."

Such a kind man! But no, I was okay. When we got to the village, I was given a little house to stay in. There were several houses where Rikbaktsa families lived and another house where there was a Brazilian couple that worked for the Missão Anchieta. The arrangement was that I was to have my meals with them and, of course, would be communicating with them in Portuguese. The rest of the time I would be trying to speak in the Rikbaktsa language, except for the moments when I'd talk to the dogs or the babies in English – or God.

Members of Wycliffe were always warned against spending too much time with speakers of the national language. Our call was to the tribes, to the ones who, without us, would have no chance of hearing about God. Learning an unwritten language was slow and laborious, so much harder than learning Portuguese. We must not get sidetracked. More than once on a Sunday afternoon, when I was taking a break from my regular work, I wondered if it would be good to go to the house of the Brazilian couple and offer to read the Bible to them. They would have been nominal Catholics with no church except when the priest came by, and probably unable to read for themselves. They might appreciate it if I went to read to them. But I thought of our mission's advice about not getting sidetracked by working in the national language, so I didn't go. A couple of years later, I heard that the man of the couple had died, and I felt so sad that I'd not taken the opportunity of reading to them and telling them more about God.

It was while I was staying there that I had my biggest spider adventure. Prior to going to Brazil I'd been the sort of person who hated killing anything, even a fly or a moth. But this time I was the only person around. I'd woken during the night, needing to go to the loo, and gone out of the house to the bushes. Coming back in, I could see by the light of my torch that there was a large tarantula in the doorway of the house. Tarantulas have a black body nearly as big as the palm of a hand with big, black, hairy legs. They also have a dangerous sting. I couldn't just step over it and pretend I'd not seen it. It was up to me to do something. I went back to the bushes and found a stick, came back and hit hard with the stick. I missed the spider – not surprising when you take into account that my eyes were tight shut at the time! But it had been near enough a blow to put the spider in battle mode. It had reared up on its legs and, if my memory hasn't exaggerated the story over the years, was actually hissing. I hit again – with my eyes open this time – and succeeded in killing it at last. I went back to my hammock, shaking but triumphant.

It was also in that village that I had one of my greatest medical successes. In the house next to mine was a family of Rikbaktsa whose father was very ill. He looked extremely thin and jaundiced and hardly ever left his hammock. In the weeks in Cuiabá before I'd come on this trip, I'd been irritated with myself because I'd spent a lot of time studying tropical illnesses instead of language – it had seemed a bit of a diversion from my main job, but now I understood why I'd been led to do that. I had read that in untreated cases of amoebic dysentery, the amoebae can migrate to the liver, causing just the symptoms I saw in him, and that it can be fatal. The treatment, however, is not difficult. Included in the medicine box of most people like us in a tropical village were ampoules of Aralen, ready to inject for severe cases of malaria. This same Aralen, injected daily for five days, is the treatment of choice for amoeba of the liver. I went round to give the first injection to my neighbour and explained that I'd be back every afternoon for five days. He was willing to try it and all went well for the first three days. On the fourth afternoon I duly filled my syringe and went round to his house. His hammock was empty. My immediate thought was, "He's died and they didn't tell me." I was shocked to the core.

But, "He'll be back," his wife consoled me. "He's just gone fishing." My only concern then was to keep the syringe clean until he got home. Oh, the joy of knowing that he was well enough to go fishing again! His wife was showing no emotion, nor did anyone else as I went round the village telling everyone. I had to rejoice alone.

We completed the course of injections and he was amazingly, wonderfully back to normal health again. Months later, when it was time for me to return to town, I realised that the people hadn't been as unemotional as I'd thought. His wife said, "Don't go. If you go, we shall all die. My man would have died if you had not been here." I had to leave, but those were words to treasure for a long time to come.

It was a good thing I went back to town. It was the time of our annual mission conference, held in a school in Goiânia. I'd been asked to sleep in a room with three of the teenage girls, to try to maintain some sort of law and order in a fairly relaxed way. I was fine about that – except that I did feel tired all the time. Was it just that I'd had malaria a number of times? One day, in a break between meetings, I went to a local supermarket, bought a bag of sweets and, to my shame, opened the bag and started eating them hungrily before I'd even paid for them. What was going on? Tired, desperate for sugar? I looked at the whites of my eyes. Yes, definitely a yellow tinge. I had hepatitis. This time I was going to be out of the tribe for quite a while.

A village outing.

CHAPTER THIRTEEN

Early Stages of Translation

1967 - 1975

After the annual mission conference I went back to Cuiabá. In the intervening years, my friends Glyn and Cynthia had borne three children and built a house on the Wycliffe plot of land outside the town. Bless them, they'd included an extra bedroom for "Auntie Joan" and there I was to stay until I was fit again. At first, they were in town too, and Cynthia did a sterling job looking after me as well as her family. Later, she and Glyn and the little boys went back to their tribe, and an American couple, who had come down to help out in Brazil for a few months, moved into the house to look after Glyn and Cynthia's eldest child, Ruth, who was about five and was going to school on the mission compound. I was glad that I was there for Ruth. We had a project going, making clothes for a doll she had. I was given scraps of cloth and wool by whoever had anything to spare, and when Ruth came in from school, she would sit on my bed and try on her dolly whatever I'd managed to make that day. I remember sometimes sitting up in bed, feeling really ill, pouring with sweat, as I tried to sew or knit. But it was all so eminently worthwhile when Ruth came in and was pleased with the addition to her doll's wardrobe. Then we'd have a discussion about what her doll needed the next day. I think I helped her; I'm sure she helped me.

During that time, I received a letter from a friend in England who had been praying for me. "You must be longing to get back to your tribe," she wrote. "We're praying you'll soon be well enough to go." To my surprise, I realised that I wasn't longing to go at all, and I began praying that God would give me the strength – physically and emotionally – to shoulder my burden again. Then one day, as I was reading the Psalms, a verse jumped out at me, God saying about his people, "I removed the burden from their shoulders; their hands were set free from the basket." Whatever could this mean? Was God saying that I wouldn't always be working in the Rikbaktsa tribe, or was it just that the burden would become less heavy as time went on? Only time would tell.

I was given no further instructions, so I could only assume that, for the time being at least, I was to continue in the tribe. Eventually I was well again and back I went, sometimes alone, sometimes with a temporary companion. It was during this time that June Morris came to keep me company – she normally worked as our mission librarian in Brasília – and I recorded a tape to send home to my parents in England. I recently rediscovered the tape and thought it might be interesting to transcribe it for you here. It is dated February 1972:

> *I'm doing something today that I don't usually do – that is, recording a tape on a day when I don't feel like it, a day when everything's going wrong! But perhaps it's worth sharing this sort of day with you as well as the happier days, so that you can understand the frustrations that can arise in living in a remote village, and so that you know how to pray for us in our need of patience and wisdom and lots of other things!*
>
> *Well, the day started by my going out, trying to do a medical round. One of the people I had to see was a woman who's covered in sores. We're all getting bitten by insects all the time, but at the moment her bites are getting infected and she has these horrible boils all over her back and legs. A few days ago we gave her some medicine for it, but she didn't take the medicine, so we decided that she had to have some of our treasured penicillin injections instead. We gave her one yesterday and one the day before, but when I went round today with the third one, she wouldn't have it. I tried to explain to her that the sores were already getting better*

and one more injection would help her to get really well, but she just refused to have any more. And, stupidly, I came away feeling thoroughly irritated and upset. I didn't know how to cope with the situation and left feeling inadequate and impatient.

And then, when I got back to our house, because it was Sunday morning I got into my hammock with my Portuguese bible and a book of Sunday school lessons ready to read some of the Word and go to Sunday school! But I don't think I'd read more than one paragraph, when somebody came to the house wanting malaria medicine. Then someone came with a cut foot that needed attention. Another woman came bringing her grubby little son who climbed into my hammock and wiped his feet over my clean Sunday blouse! You know the sort of day. And then she wasn't feeling well and asked me to go down to the river and get water for her. And, unaccountably, I felt irritated again. I just felt that I don't have enough love or patience to do the job here that God has given me to do. So would you pray that God will give us all the qualities of character that we need? We must love these people with God's kind of love, the kind of love that is patient and kind.

As I'm talking to you now, you can probably hear in the background the voices of other people. There are a group of women in the house, watching me, asking what I'm doing, chatting to one another. Normally we're delighted that people come to our house so readily and that we have so many friends here. But there are times when I'd love to escape for a few hours and have a little peace. Sometimes though, when we're feeling at the end of our tether, it seems as if God arranges a day for us when everybody goes out for a day's hunting and we can have a few hours of quiet. We really appreciate a day like that from time to time.

But I mustn't go on about the difficulties, because in the weeks that June and I have been here we've felt really aware of God working in the village. And in us too. We feel that the work here is getting to an exciting stage. It does look as if we'll be able to start translating in a few months' time. This is hugely encouraging after the years of making such very slow progress in the language. One thing that makes me feel like that is the way that God has obviously changed the situation regarding language helpers. You know how, in the early days when we were here, we often asked you to pray for local people to help us learn the language because, although they were friendly enough, they didn't seem to realise that we needed someone to come round daily to help us. But since I've been back this time, there's been one man – his name translated to English is "Red Macaw" – who's been coming round just about every day and sometimes twice a day to teach me. I'm beginning to feel that with his help, I'm actually starting to make some progress.

And soon after I got back, he told me that he wanted to see Cuiabá. I immediately thought of the times when we have what we call "workshops" in town, when several of us missionaries get together for a few weeks of intensive working on our different languages. And thinking of this I said, "Yes, I will take you to Cuiabá one day, because I want you to come and teach me more of your language." He said that he will come and was eager to know how soon it would be.

Soon after this I was telling him some Bible stories and I realised that as I was trying in my stumbling and halting way, perhaps using gestures or pointing at pictures to explain what needed to be said, he was giving it back to me in correct flowing Rikbaktsa language. And this just thrilled me, because it's exactly what we need when we come to doing any formal Bible translation. We need someone who will grasp the idea of what a verse means and will give it back to us accurately in their own language. Exactly what Red Macaw was doing!

Then, another day, we had a houseful of men here and, in response to their questions, I was talking to them about what will happen to me when I die. I said I'm going to be with Jesus in the sky, and tried to explain that my body would be buried but that my spirit would be with Jesus. But I didn't know the word for "spirit". However, as I tried to explain, Red Macaw got the idea of what I was trying to say and explained it to the other men, using their word for "spirit". I began to feel sure that God has been preparing him to be our translation helper in coming days. So, although I don't feel that my command of the language is enough to start translation, I do believe that God has been preparing him, and I hope to begin working on some of the stories from the Gospels before the end of this year. In July, there's to be a translation workshop in Cuiabá, and I'd like to take Red Macaw to town then to begin preparing a "Life of Christ" in Rikbaktsa. Please pray that I won't begin too soon and make serious mistakes, but that if it is what God wants, I won't be afraid to start.

Another very encouraging thing about this session in the tribe has been that several of the men are extremely interested in learning to read. I wish you could come here one evening and be in the house with us to see how eagerly they gather in the light of the oil lamp and practise writing on their blackboards the words that they are learning to read, how keen they are to help one another and to explain things to one another. Several of them are making quite good progress and can now recognise lots of words and even some syllables and letters. I feel that here, again, God is preparing them so that when some parts of the Bible are available in their language, some of the men will be ready to read them. Ideally, we should have had reading primers available by now, the sort of books that we all learned to read by when we were young, but I haven't had time to prepare these and we're still working from charts and flash cards. This is something else we need to be thinking about and working towards in the next few months.

Eventually, Sheila's home situation was such that she was able to return from England and take up work in the tribe again. Actually, it was she who took over the responsibility for the reading primers, and began to function again as a vital part of the team. It really is a two-man job!

We began by trying to do a rough paraphrase of some of the stories about Jesus in the Bible. The choice of story depended not on its theological importance but on what stories we had enough vocabulary for! One of the first was the account of the healing of the blind man, Bartimaeus. We had a Ladybird book with a simplified version of that story and lots of pictures to help us get the story across. I had figured out how to tell in the vernacular what happened: the blind man at the roadside hearing Jesus and his followers passing by; the blind man shouting to Jesus to help him; Jesus stopping and asking Bartimaeus to come to him; Jesus saying, "You can see;" the blind man seeing.

One day a Rikbaktsa family came to our house for medicine for a baby who had a fever. After we had given the required medicine, the father and mother and big brother, who must have been about five years old, sat on the floor for a chat. I got out the Ladybird book, sat on the floor with them and told them the story I'd been practising. The father couldn't figure it out. He was saying to his wife, "I thought she said he was blind."

I interrupted, "Yes, he was blind. But then Jesus spoke, and after that he could see. After Jesus spoke, he was healed. He wasn't blind anymore."

The five-year-old didn't need any more explanation. He was dancing round our house, stamping his right foot to provide the rhythm in the normal Rikbaktsa fashion, and singing his own little song:

Sesusi zihyrizik zorowy. Sesusi zihyrizik zorowy.[2]

This was probably the first Rikbaktsa praise song ever composed. My heart sang with him.

Music and dance are a big part of Rikbaktsa life, the rhythm always provided by stamping the right foot, usually with a cord of nutshells tied round that ankle. The rest of the music is provided by wind instruments – hollow tubes of bamboo with a reed in one end to blow or nose flutes made from two concave pieces of gourd stuck together

---

[2] Jesus healed his eyes. Jesus healed his eyes.

with beeswax. One of the pieces of gourd has three holes bored in it, air is breathed into one of the holes and a variety of delicate little whistling notes is made by covering or uncovering the other two holes. The dancers dress in elaborate feather headdresses, their bodies painted with red and black colours made from crushed berries and wood-ash. Sometimes they add white decorations made from the down feathers of birds. It is the men who have the skills for making the musical instruments and headdresses. The women's job is to provide the drink – huge pots of maize drink and smaller pots of "zaru", made of well-chewed Brazil nuts. At the time of the maize harvest, the dancing could go on for days. The men would dance for hours on end, and when they were tired, the women would take over for a while. Always with the fear that if they didn't dance enough, there would be no harvest next year. A line of stamping people, blowing their instruments, round and round the village, in and out of the houses, until they were exhausted. Then, tomorrow and tomorrow, more of the same. It was colourful, beautiful, well organised, but also, I felt, relentless and desperate.

One evening, when I was watching them dancing, one of the older men left the line of dancers and came and sat down for a rest on the log beside me. He began telling me the latest gossip of the village, that one of the women had been having an affair with someone else and her husband was *very* angry. I took the opportunity to tell him that Jesus said we should be married to only one person and stay with that person all the time. That way people wouldn't need to feel jealous and angry. "Ah," he replied, "Jesus really knows." It interested me to see again that God's wisdom is relevant to all cultures.

I struggled to get their music. There were different tunes that they could all recognise, but which sounded very similar to me. One day I took my tape recorder to the house of a lame old man they called Capitão (Portuguese for "captain"). I thought if he sang a song or two for me to record and I listened enough times, I might be able to "hear" the different tunes. I don't think I was successful in that, but I did learn something of importance that day. In his younger days, he had once been so ill that he had not moved from his hammock for weeks, and the muscles in his legs had atrophied. Now he could only move around by sitting on the ground and propelling himself forward by taking his weight on his arms. For that reason, he could not get down to the river without great difficulty and hence washed only very rarely. That day, when I arrived with my tape recorder, he said, "Go to the river. Get me some water," and indicated the water pot he wanted me to fill. I walked down to the river, quite crossly. I'm ashamed to say that I was thinking of all the years of education I'd had and feeling seriously affronted that a smelly old man should be bossing me around. I arrived at the river's edge, and knelt down on the bank to fill his water pot. Was it the act of kneeling that suddenly made me see the situation in a totally different light? Maybe so. Because I was immediately transformed. I was thinking now about Jesus "humbling himself and becoming obedient" and, in comparison, the ugliness of my pride and my wanting to be someone. I asked God's forgiveness, filled the water pot and carried it back up to the old man's house, a different woman.

I remember another incident in that village that taught me a spiritual lesson. There were often several children in our house sheltering from the gnats outside, chatting or waiting to go with us for our daily swim in the river. One of the ones who was always there was Tabawy, a happy, outgoing girl about ten years old. One day she was looking through our box of medicines, especially interested in a bottle of iodine. I asked her to put it down because I didn't want anything to be wasted, and then went to attend to something cooking on our mud stove. When I came back, some of the children were still there but Tabawy had gone. And there was a puddle of red iodine rapidly disappearing in the dusty earth floor. We didn't do anything about it that day, assuming that she'd be back and we could speak to her about it then. But she didn't come the next day, or the next. And when we went to her house, she wasn't there either. In the end, it dawned on us that much more important than the loss of the iodine was the loss of a friendly relationship with Tabawy. We found one of our few tablets of scented soap, took it to her house and asked her mother to give it to Tabawy when she came in. The next day, when the children came round to our house, Tabawy came too. There was no mention of the soap and no mention of the iodine, but we were friends again. I didn't understand it at the time. With my logical mind, I don't understand it even now. But there seems to be a profound spiritual truth here: when the aggrieved party in a dispute makes a generous or loving gesture, healing of the relationship can happen. It's a tiny echo of how the God whom we've ignored or even disobeyed treats us.

Around the same time, one of the neighbouring rubber tappers called in one day needing medicine. He was quite chatty and told me proudly that he'd had a whole year of schooling. Had I ever been to school, he wanted to know, and for how long? I was embarrassed about the inequality of his opportunities compared with mine. "Oh, we're very lucky in our country," I said casually. "We all get the chance of going to school." And, without saying how long I'd been able to study, I began to ask him about his school and whether he'd enjoyed the experience.

We saw something of our Portuguese-speaking neighbours from time to time. Once, during the period when Sheila was back in England, one of the rubber tappers began to come quite frequently. One day he would need malaria medicine, the next time he'd have run out of rice, it would then be sugar for his coffee, and so on. I just thought he was tired of being without someone to talk to, and was making every excuse to row up the river and have a chat. But the Rikbaktsa men had a different interpretation of the situation.

"Do you like that man coming to see you?" they asked.

I had to be honest. "No, not really."

"Don't worry," they said. "Next time he comes, we'll kill him for you." That seemed a bit drastic!

But I had another suggestion. "No. Next time he comes, just send all the children round to my house."

So, the following day he was only just walking up the path from the river, when our house was suddenly full of children of all ages, milling around, sitting on the box where he usually sat, and making any conversation impossible. He took his malaria tablets, left immediately and didn't come back for a long time. The Pied Piper method had worked well!

One very positive contact with our Portuguese-speaking neighbours was one Christmas Day when I was in our village with Jacky, a friend who normally worked in a tribe in the Xingu National Park. A young man from the south of Brazil, Arnildo, sent out by a Lutheran mission, was on his own, so we invited him to have lunch with us. It would be nothing like a Christmas dinner at home, but we'd do the best that we could. He suggested that in the morning he would take us in the motorboat to visit some of our Portuguese-speaking neighbours. The nearest family were a rubber tapper and his wife and two children, who had an elderly rubber tapper, Sr. Manuel, living with them and helping them out. It was a beautiful day and we all felt in holiday mood as we went along the river. When we got there, the two men were sitting in the house listening to the radio. "We've not gone to work today," they said. "It's Christmas Day. We think it's some sort of Saint's Day."

We had searched our belongings and had come up with only a tablet of scented soap for the lady of the house and some sweets for the others. So we presented our little gifts, they made us a "cafezinho" – a small cup of strong, sweet black coffee – and we sat down to chat. Arnildo had brought his Portuguese bible, and he said, "You're right to think it's some sort of Saint's Day. It's the day when we remember that Jesus Christ was born. Do you want to hear all about it from the Bible?" They did and he read it to them, stopping from time to time to explain. Then we prayed for them all and began to take our leave.

Sr. Manuel followed us as we went down the path to where the boat was moored. "Could there be any hope for a man like me?" he asked. It was well known along the river that Sr. Manuel was there because he had murdered someone back in town.

"Sr. Manuel," we said, "there is hope for every single one of us. The Jesus Christ that Arnildo has been telling you about, he grew up to be a perfect man, but died on a cross to pay for the sins of the whole world – yours and mine and everybody's. If we trust in him, we can be forgiven."

What an unusual opportunity! What a memorable Christmas Day!

One earlier Christmas, Padre Edgar had suggested that we have a Christmas service together, where he would speak in Portuguese and we would tell the story in the Rikbaktsa language. Sadly, we had to say that we were not ready. We were afraid of saying something wrong and inadvertently giving the wrong impression. When you're talking about God, it's too important to allow any mistakes. But gradually, as time went on, we increased the number of Bible stories that we could tell with a fair degree of confidence, and we planned to produce a slim book of such stories as a "Life of Christ" in their language. They loved the story of Jesus standing up in the boat and telling the wind and waves to be quiet. They enjoyed hearing about Zacchaeus climbing the tree in order to see Jesus. And they loved the fact that in Bible picture books Jesus is shown with long hair. That made him, not a "civilizado", but one of them!

One evening when a large group of men were in our house, we tried to tell them the story of the crucifixion. They had heard, by now, quite a lot about the good things Jesus did – the people he helped, the power he showed, and they knew that praying to him had brought good results for them personally. So to think about the cruelty of those who hated him and told lies about him, beat and killed him – this all shocked them deeply. They checked that we had said that he had died, their faces full of shock and grief. It was so wonderful to be able to say that wasn't the end of the story, and to tell them that he came back to life and will live forever.

Having got that far, I was eager, before I went back to England for my next home leave, to find a way of telling them that God loves us. We had words for fear, happiness and sadness, but neither of us had heard a word that seemed to mean love. Then one day a mother brought a sick baby to us and was quite tearful.

"Don't cry," I said. "Your baby will soon be well again."

"I'm crying because I ______ my baby."

Could this be the word we were looking for? We went round the houses asking, "Do you ______ your husband? Your child? Your mother? Your baby?"

They laughed at the use of this word to describe how they might feel about an adult or an older child. But, yes, they were all comfortable to use it about how they felt for a baby or a small child. It must describe the feeling of a parent for someone small and helpless. Clearly we couldn't use this word for our love of God, but it might work well for his love for us.

I was still working on this when I left the tribe to go home to the UK. We were at the airstrip at one of the villages of the Missão Anchieta and as we waited for the plane to arrive, I was chatting with some of the women. I tried out my translation for John chapter 3, verse 16, aiming to say that God loved everyone in the world so much that he gave his only son.

One of the women didn't get it. "He doesn't love me," she said, "because I've never met him."

Her friend wasn't so adamant. "I think perhaps he does love me. You remember when I was ill, Joan talked to him about me? And see, I'm better."

How exciting! Words and experience fitting together, she was embarking on her journey of discovering God.

Showing off the arrows he has made.

CHAPTER FOURTEEN

A Total Change of Direction

1975

I was continuing on my journey with God. This time I wasn't just going out to Cuiabá. I was on my way back to England, to continue my studies in Linguistics at Reading University, and to find out from God whether I was still working in the place where he wanted me to be.

The verse about God taking my shoulder from the burden was still hovering at the back of my mind. Before I left Brazil, I spoke to the field director of Wycliffe. "Jim, if anyone comes along who'd be a suitable colleague for Sheila, don't hesitate to send her to the Rikbaktsa. I've a feeling I may not be coming back."

He didn't want to hear that. "You're just not well, Joan. Hepatitis and malaria have worn you out. You'll feel very different after a few months at home."

I didn't think it was that, but time would tell.

I was thirty-eight years old, moving rapidly into middle age. Back on staff at the Summer Institute of Linguistics that year, teaching language learning to a whole new bunch of missionary recruits, I was amused one mealtime when the conversation came round to World War 2 to realise that I was the only person at the table who'd been alive during the war. "Sorry, folks. Just make allowance for an old lady reminiscing!"

Thirty-eight years old and still single. Over the years there had been possibilities, men I'd liked, men who had liked me, one friendship that had gone too far; but there had always been a good reason not to pursue any of these friendships. He's too old or he's too young, our goals in life are too different or he's called to a different part of the world from me or he's not a Christian. The friendship that had caused me the most tears was with an American eight years younger than me and, more importantly, an atheist – clearly he could be nothing more to me than a dear friend. Now, I was starting to think, "I'm just not going to get married. Help me, Lord, to be content with whatever you want for me." I remembered in my schooldays saying to a friend that when I grew up and got married – it had seemed obvious in those days that I would marry – I was going to have four children, all boys. I thought of that ruefully now. That was one daydream that wasn't going to happen.

After the summer, I continued living at the Wycliffe Centre near High Wycombe, to be within easy reach of Reading University. Some days I went to Reading, some days I studied in my room, and most weekends I was away visiting churches up and down the country, talking about the work of Wycliffe Bible Translators, and especially Brazil and the Rikbaktsa people. Everywhere I went people asked me, "When are you going back?" and always I replied, "Next year," but whenever I said that, there was that huge question mark in my mind. I felt almost as if I was telling a lie.

Early the next spring other possible work opportunities began to crop up. Wycliffe was starting work in Cameroon, West Africa. Some new, young members were preparing to go, but there was a need for someone with a bit more experience to go and work with them. Would I consider it? However, when the people in the personnel office heard that, they said, "If Joan's not going back to Brazil, we want her here. We need someone who has experience overseas to chat with returning missionaries about their difficulties." I was flattered by both these offers. I hadn't realised before that being middle-aged opens doors to new kinds of opportunities! Writing letters to my supporters, I mentioned that there was the possibility of working with Wycliffe in another country or in the office at home instead of going back to Brazil, and asked them to pray that I'd make the right decision.

One of these letters went to Philip Kearney. He was now the minister of a Baptist Church in Leicestershire. His wife, Ann, had died the previous year in her early thirties after some years of debilitating illness, leaving him with three young boys. But, bless him, he'd continued praying for me and sending the occasional monetary gift, just as they had done all the time I'd been overseas. I'd added a note in the letter to Philip, not only thanking him for the gift but saying also something like, "And how are you? I pray for you often in the struggle of being responsible for the family and the church on your own." His reply was a total surprise. He was struggling and he wanted us to meet up as soon as possible, implying that there might be a future for us together. He has said since that he thought I was wedded to Brazil but if that was in question, maybe... I wrote back saying I was still confused by all the doors that were opening for me, and I didn't think we should meet until I was sure whether God wanted me back in Brazil or not.

It was Easter time and I went home to my parents, now living in Lytham St. Annes, feeling sure I'd get some guidance during the holidays. But no. After that fortnight, back at the Wycliffe Centre, I was feeling under huge pressure. So many people needed a reply from me, and I'd already kept them waiting too long. Then one night I read a paraphrase of the verse, "But when you ask, you must believe and not doubt." The paraphrase read, "Ask, fully expecting that God will give you an answer." Maybe that's where I'd been going wrong, maybe I hadn't "fully expected"? So I prayed, "Please show me tomorrow and, so that I can't get it wrong, please show me the same answer in three different ways – through a letter, through something I'll read in the Bible, and through something someone will say to me." The next morning, I woke feeling rather nervous about it all. I'd never prayed that way before. It's not usual to tie God down to a certain day. But it was done now.

My morning Bible reading was from the book of Proverbs. There was no one sentence to guide me, but there was a lot about the sort of man that God approves of: a kind man, a generous man, someone who is not proud. That sounded like Philip – could God be saying that I was meant to marry him?

I went to see if there was any mail for me. There was a card from a young Dutch missionary couple I knew, announcing the birth of their first baby, a little boy. And the card was headed, "Sons are a heritage from the Lord." Sons? If I married Philip I would be stepmum to three young boys. This was especially significant. The week before, I had again read the verse that took me to Brazil: "He chose our inheritance for us." It had left me bewildered. Was God reminding me that he'd already chosen Brazil? Or was there now another inheritance? When I got the birth announcement card that morning, I thought, "inheritance – heritage – sons..."

Throughout the day, I was listening intently to every conversation. My third strand of guidance was going to be through what someone said. But each conversation had nothing relating to West Africa or South America, and nothing about personnel work or marriage. Until quite late in the evening. We'd had a prayer meeting in someone's home on the base and, as we were standing around chatting and drinking cocoa at the end, a visitor from Leicestershire arrived, the Rev. Harry Sutton. He had come down to lend his church's large van to Wycliffe. I had known him as a council member when I was a student at BBI and now, as he joined us for cocoa, I went over to say hello and have a chat. I asked after the wellbeing of various old BBI students from his area, including Philip.

And then he said to me, "What about you, Joan? When are you going back to Brazil?"

I told him the predicament I was in. "I could go back to Brazil, or Wycliffe are offering me two other possible fields of service, or there's a minister in this country who's interested in marrying me. I just don't know what God wants."

The answer surprised him as well as me. "Marriage is the normal thing," he said.

In the years afterwards, he told me that he couldn't believe the words that were coming out of his mouth. He had always thought of the single-woman missionary as being like a nun, the prototype of dedication to God. But shortly before that conversation with me, he had been in India visiting several mission stations and almost wherever he went, different single women had come to him for a pastoral chat, confiding in him their struggle with loneliness and dissatisfaction. Hence now his totally unexpected response: "Marriage is the normal thing." I'd had my three answers from God.

I went back to my room bowled over by it all. And as I read Daily Light before I went to sleep, there was a final confirmation: "The Lord bestows favour and honour. No good thing does he withhold from those whose walk is blameless." That had been a difficult verse for me through my single years. Marriage is a good thing. Was God saying I wasn't living in a blameless way? Where was I going wrong? But now it was abundantly clear. God, after all this time, was going to give me the gift of a husband.

It was a Thursday night. On Friday I was going away to be the speaker at a church's missionary weekend and stay there with a couple I'd not met before. It wouldn't be good to ask to use their phone for a long-distance call. I decided to phone Philip when I got back on Sunday evening. Meanwhile, God was speaking to him too. This is his story.

> *Yes, I was indeed struggling! My wife, Ann, died after three years of alternating monthly stays in hospital or at home. We had three lively sons – identical twins, Andrew and Timothy, just about to celebrate their fifth birthday, and their eight-and-a-half-year-old brother, Jonathan. As a pastor in a large rural village, it was more than a full-time job, and I was immensely grateful for a God-given single lady church member, who had very recently retired from a lifetime in the Leicester hosiery industry. Kathleen became a wonderful source of love for the boys and a very practical housekeeper for us all.*
>
> *People were very kind in those days, including me when inviting friends round for a meal or a social evening. However, in those groups of couples I often found it difficult. I was the odd-one out – now a widower, seen as a possible answer to the prayers of at least one single lady in the church! At thirty-five years of age, I could not consider the thought that God's plan for me would be to remain a single parent with three motherless sons. I reflect on that period of my life as being one of the most difficult experiences I have ever faced and, had it not been for the children, would have resigned as a pastor and... but I can't begin to think of where I might have gone or what employment I would have found.*
>
> *I was struggling – spiritually, emotionally and in my work as a pastor. And it wasn't a help when a Christian friend one day explained to me that a small group in the church felt my*

preaching over recent months was proving of no help to them!

And so, to pick up the story where Joan has paused, I naively thought that it was she who needed to know clearly what God was saying about our future. For her, if we married, it would be a complete change of calling. For me, even though it would bring big changes at home, it would be continuing in the same house and the same job. And so the weeks went on. But God wisely knew that I also would need a clear indication if his plan was for Joan and me to be married. However, one Saturday I decided to write a letter to Joan saying that if God was calling her to go back to Brazil or whatever else He had in mind for her, I released her from any thoughts of our future together. Sunday mail collections took place in those days, so I waited until the Sunday morning to sign off the letter and post it.

That very morning, my daily Bible readings schedule took me to the story of Abraham sending his servant to find a wife for Isaac, Abraham's son. The servant arrives at Rachel's house and puts the question to Rachel's father. His response is simply, "We cannot say yes or no. The thing proceeds from the Lord." Those words jumped out of the page at me in a way I don't remember another Bible verse ever doing. I knew immediately that this was my answer from God and that Joan, by then, would have her answer too. I added a very brief postscript to my letter saying that God had spoken to me and I believed she would also have received God's leading for her future. No further details. The letter was posted on my way to lead the morning service at church.

Philip's letter was posted but, of course, I hadn't received it when I got back to the Wycliffe Centre that night and phoned him. It was an extraordinary situation to be in. We hadn't met since I'd been in England four years earlier and there had never been any "in love" relationship between us, but we had known one another fairly well and had been friends since we had been students together more than ten years before. And now we both knew that it was God's plan that we should get married. We arranged to meet up the following Friday in Banbury. I'd go up on the train, Philip would drive down while the boys were at school, and we'd meet and talk and have lunch together to make some plans.

As it happened, Philip's car was out of action the next Friday. He went to one of the couples in the church who were very generous in lending their cars and asked to borrow one for a trip down to Banbury. The wife teased him, "Ah, off to Banbury Cross to see a fine lady upon a white horse, are we?" No white horse – I came by British Rail. And there was nothing of the fine lady about it. I was taking my coat off and putting it on again, looking at my watch every few seconds, and just not knowing what to do or think. I was so nervous, I thought that if the train had been going beyond Banbury, I might have stayed on it! But Banbury was the terminus, so I got off and there was Philip waiting on the platform for me. I don't remember a lot about that day, but I do remember Philip's hand, warm and strong, as we walked up the stairs to the station exit holding hands.

One of the first things we talked about was where we would live. I think Philip wondered whether I could still work with Wycliffe in some capacity, not in the forests of Brazil but maybe in some support role in this country. But I couldn't see how that was possible. It was hard enough for the boys to have lost their own mum, and now they were having a stepmum foisted on them, I didn't want to give them the added stress of moving from home and school, friends and relatives as well. I thought we should settle in Fleckney. And I think Philip was pleased with that decision. We arranged to meet again the following Friday and get engaged. We arranged for me to go to Fleckney, his village in Leicestershire, and meet the boys and the church. We fixed some dates for him to meet my parents, Bryan and Janet, and Hilary and her husband, Harold. And we began to think about a wedding that summer, only a couple of months away. Looking back now, it seems like a whirlwind. Then it seemed normal – we'd had our instructions from God and had only to carry them out step by step.

That first weekend in Fleckney was not easy. I went up by coach, and Philip and the boys were at the bus stop to welcome me. Jonathan's first conversational gambit was to ask me what size of shoes I take! It turned out that he had just gone into size 5 and was hoping that we'd be the same. Sadly mine are size 8, so it took him a year or two to catch up! The twins, Andrew and Timothy, were quiet, weighing me up. I can't imagine now why I didn't talk to them all more and begin to build a proper relationship. I suppose I felt out of place and was trying to slide into their lives unnoticed! I stayed with Kathleen, the kind lady who'd been like an unpaid housekeeper for Philip. When I was settled in there, and Philip went up to the bathroom, he told me later that he'd looked under my pillow to see what kind of nightgown I wore. It was a red one that I'd taken from the "boutique", a store of second-hand clothes at the Wycliffe Centre for people coming back from overseas. I never asked how he'd felt about the red nightie – it was quite a risk for him, marrying a middle-aged spinster!

Meeting the church was something else. Only Eric, the church secretary, and Kathleen knew that their minister had become engaged. After giving out the notices for that week, Eric said, "I'm happy to say that I have a special announcement to make. Our minister, Philip, has just become engaged to Joan, and she is with us this morning." The balcony of that little village chapel was in serious danger, Eric said afterwards, as all the young people up there leaned over, eager to see this strange woman about to move into their village! Most of the church were welcoming, but tentative, understandably. After the evening service, I was asked to speak about my life in Brazil, but I quickly realised that people weren't really interested in Brazil – they wanted to know whether I'd look after Philip and the boys properly and what sort of minister's wife I was going to be!

I had to let all my friends and supporters know, to tell the university that I wouldn't be finishing my thesis, and to tell the folks at Wycliffe that I'd be leaving. Reactions were very varied. Some people thought I was opting out of God's call, letting down the mission, the tribe, even the supporters who had prayed for me and provided finances for me for the last ten years. I could see their viewpoint, and was so very glad that we had waited until we knew that we were doing what God wanted. One Wycliffe leader said that the training and experience I'd been given were a preparation for my future service in the mission, and that would now be wasted. I said I couldn't agree – most of us had been well qualified in other fields before we became missionaries – but God sometimes moves us on into something totally different. I see that even more clearly now. His teaching of us isn't just knowledge in our heads. So often what matters is the experience in our hearts, what God is building into our characters. My journey through life has been a lot like schooling. You get to the top of the primary school and feel comfortable and confident, but then there's the secondary school – you're one of the young ones again, new and strange and a bit scared! As God has moved me from situation to situation, I know well those months or years of readjustment, re-learning, feeling terribly insecure.

Certainly leaving Wycliffe and becoming a minister's wife was one of those times for me. We were married in June 1975 – if it hadn't been for my mum and Hilary making lots of the practical arrangements, I can't imagine what would have happened! They even arranged for me to have my hair done at a hairdresser's the morning of the wedding – I'd never have thought of that! Then Philip and I had a lovely week together in the Isle of Skye, before getting back to Fleckney, to my new norm.

Wedding – our new family

Chapter Fifteen

Life as a Housewife and Mum

1975 - 1979

I don't know where to start to tell you about the things I found hard. But you know me quite well by now. You know I like being on my own and having my own space. And you know that I'm not by nature a homemaker, and care very little what things look like. Both these aspects of my character made life seriously difficult for me in those early days. My own space? It became a luxury to go to the bathroom. Often I'd pray there, just feeling for a few moments that I could be myself and not have to be nice to anybody! Sometimes the pantry was a place of retreat, too. When we had visitors and I was trying to prepare a meal for them, I'd sometimes hide for a second in the pantry telling God I needed his help to get this show on the road! There were times at the weekend when we'd be going out somewhere with the boys and I'd opt to stay in and bake a cake for tea, but I began to realise that this was unfair to Philip. When Ann had been ill and after her death, he had so wanted to be a complete family again. I needed to try to fill that lack now.

What about the difficulty of my not being a good housewife? Or a good cook? Certain incidents stand out in my mind. One was when Ann's parents were coming to tea. I made a lovely cherry cake and, as a final flourish, sprinkled some sugar crystals on as a topping, but the "sugar crystals" turned out to be rock salt and, in the process of baking, had drifted down through the cake, making it so salty as to be totally inedible! We laugh now. At the time I was mortified.

Another memory concerns our black piano. A lady from the church called in one day and absentmindedly ran a finger in the dust on top of the piano. Nowadays I'd laugh and say, "Oops, failed again!" But then I felt an utter failure. I even began to wonder if God had made a mistake in calling me to this new sphere of service. Ann had been pretty; I know I'm not. When she was well, Ann had been a meticulous housewife; I get by with the minimum of cleaning and dusting. She was the real mother of the boys; I felt I was a very poor substitute. One day one of the twins said something cute and Philip looked at me expecting me to be sharing his enjoyment of the moment, but I had to switch on a smile a moment too late. Being a step-parent is not easy. I began to sink into depression. All the things I was any good at were no use to me now. Nobody cared that I could speak Portuguese, or write down and analyse an unwritten language, or lecture in Linguistics! Everything I was responsible for now was new and difficult for me.

We had a week of special evangelistic meetings in the church with Rev. Brian Gilbert as the speaker. The first evening, Philip arranged a babysitter so that I could go to the church too. At the end, Brian asked those who needed God's help in their life to go forward and be prayed with. He was really meaning people for whom it was the first time they'd asked God for help, and he was surprised that I went out wanting someone to pray with me. One of the women in the church joined me. "What do you want me to pray for, Joan?" she asked.

I could reply only, "I'm so, so tired."

One night I dreamed that Ann came back. I was pleased and, to save any embarrassment, decided that I'd just leave without saying goodbye to anyone. In my dream, I set off to walk along the canal to Leicester thinking how happy they'd all be without me. That was just a dream; the reality was that I was still in Fleckney, still learning to cope with my new life.

At breakfast time one morning there was a phone call from a man in the church saying that his wife was ill with depression. Would Philip pop round and see her and have a chat? So when Philip had taken the boys to school, he went straight round to visit her. When he got back, he found me washing up, tears dripping off my chin into the sink, eaten up with self-pity because he'd gone off to help someone else when I needed him to help me. Ugh, self-pity is such an ugly emotion! I had to go to the doctor and get some medication to make life a little easier for us all.

You must not imagine that I was always in tears, though. There are happy memories too. I'm a big fan of fruit and vegetables, and it was a joy to me to see Andy and Tim change from little lads who always seemed to have runny noses, into healthy youngsters who hardly ever had a day off school. It was a joy, too, to see how the boys calmed down. With an ill mother, their lives had been quite stressful, and one of the ways they'd reacted was by being constantly restless and on the go. When they came in from school, it was our custom to have a drink of milk and a biscuit ready. My expectation was that they would sit down or at least stand still for their snack, but no, they'd march backwards and forwards in the kitchen, never still for a second.

Andy told me once that when he started school, the teacher was cross because he'd get up from his chair and run around the classroom.

"Why do you think you did that?"

"I don't know. But I don't run around now."

They were never placid children – it wasn't in their nature – but they did begin to feel calmer and that was an encouragement to me.

And we had some great outings. At first, when we had longish car journeys, the boys would get bored and begin to squabble and argue. Later we found that it was a good time for guessing games, or when we were on our way to my parents' at Lytham St. Annes, there would be a sweet for the first person to see Blackpool Tower (or, as it usually turned out, a sweet for everyone and two for the first one who'd seen the tower). I read a lot of books to them on car journeys – Roald Dahl, C.S. Lewis and Enid Blyton. Jon was already a good reader when I came along. Andy and Tim cut their literary teeth on "Famous Five" books. There were pleasures that we could share together.

I remember one wonderful day out in London. We left early in the morning and drove to Stanstead, where we left the car and caught the tube into the city centre. On the Underground we met Rev. Dr David Russell, who was then the general secretary of the Baptist Union. Philip introduced himself and had a chat. As we were leaving, Dr Russell said to me, "Make the most of these years. They pass so quickly." He couldn't have said anything more helpful to me at that time. That morning we saw the changing of the guard, had a look at Buckingham

Palace and ate our picnic lunch in Green Park. Are the birds there still as tame? That day chaffinches came to share our picnic and were even sitting on our hands and pecking our sandwiches as we lifted the bread to our mouths! (That was probably when Tim became interested in birds. When he was recovering from chicken pox around that time, he spent ages at the bedroom window with binoculars watching the birds in the garden below. He even joined the Leicester Young Ornithologists for a while and used to meet up with them for bird-watching walks around the area.)

In the afternoon of our day in London we had a look round Harrods. I was intrigued to see how the other half lives, looking at child-sized cars and caravans "to be driven on private estates only"! The boys' big moment was seeing someone being arrested by store-detectives for shoplifting. Then we went to the department where there were hand-made Belgian chocolates. We've never had a lot of money, so we checked with the assistant how much five chocolates would cost. She weighed them and put them in a little pink-and-white striped drawstring bag. We carried it to the stairwell where there was nobody around, and felt rich and decadent as we enjoyed one each!

The twins were doing well. They had only known Ann ill, so there had not been a major change for them to get used to, and throughout the difficult years they had always had one another. Jon, I think, was the one who had suffered the most. He remembered her as being a very sweet and adoring mother when he was small. But when she had twin babies to cope with as well, and when she became very ill and was struggling to keep going at all, Jon's life was very different. Then she died. One day in the playground at school some other boys spoke to him about his mother's death and he attacked them with furious fists. There was a pain in him that he couldn't speak about. If we mentioned her, or Philip showed slides with Ann on, Jon would go out of the room. I think he'd have liked me to be the sweet and adoring person that Ann had been when he was tiny, but I couldn't. It must have seemed to him like a cold north wind blowing in his life as I came in brisk and bracing and wanting them to grow up into strong men. Psychologists say that sometimes children feel that it would be disloyal to their real parent to accept a step-parent. Perhaps there was something of that in the mix too – I don't know. I just know that we both struggled with our relationship and it was years – he was almost grown-up – before we became real friends.

And Philip? How was he? I had underestimated the suffering of all the family during the years of Ann's illness. I suppose that I'd imagined, without putting it into words, "Yes, it's been a very tough time for them all, but in a few months we'll be a normal, happy family." How stupid was that! There were "thoughts that do often lie too deep for tears"[3], wounds from feeling bewildered, inadequate, unable to help. Philip had changed from the light-hearted teasing young man I'd known at college into someone much more mature, but with a sense of failure, with thoughts and feelings he didn't know how to express. It wasn't an easy time for any of us.

But in the church God was beginning to do amazing things. The young woman who lived next door had already become a Christian. It wasn't long before her husband followed suit. And at the week of special meetings with Brian Gilbert, a young couple who'd been looking for answers with Jehovah's Witnesses both made a commitment to Christ, as did a lady who'd not long been in the village, as well as another young woman whose husband soon did the same. That continued for several years, not hundreds of people becoming Christians, but a steady growth by ones and twos. Philip was minister of that church for over twenty years altogether, and the number of church members went from about thirty to around a hundred, even after many had moved to jobs in other parts of the country. We could hardly believe what God was doing. We were very aware of our own weakness, but God was building a team of committed people who were making an impact for good in the area. Maybe it's just more evidence of the fact that God's power is strongest when we are weak.[4]

Philip was working very hard in the church. One week we added up and found that he'd done over seventy hours – that wasn't unusual. Sermon preparation, church services, meetings, visiting people who were ill or lonely or just needed to chat over a problem – all these things took time. My job was to be the backup and to try to keep things running smoothly on the home front. Philip always tried to be in by 10pm to see the news. That was our time. The boys were in bed, the

---

[3] From *Ode on Intimations of Immortality;* Wordsworth.
[4] See 2 Corinthians 12:9.

phone wasn't going to ring and we could sit peacefully with an evening drink, hold hands and watch TV or talk about the events of the day. We had other times just for us. Sometimes, on a Monday, Philip tried to take time off and we'd go to Leicester and have lunch in a Chinese restaurant we both liked. Occasionally we'd be invited out to Philip's friends' for a meal.

When we got back from one such evening out, Kathleen, who'd been babysitting for us, said that a distraught young man had been at the door and that when he heard that Philip wasn't in, he'd paced up and down the pavement for a while, waiting for us to come back. Philip guessed who it was and, when he'd taken Kathleen home, went to the young man's house. There was no reply to his ring at the doorbell, so he looked through a gap in the curtains of the living room, saw the gas fire full on and the young man slumped unconscious in a chair. Mercifully, the key was in the door, so Philip went in to the heat and a strong smell of medication. He phoned 999 and the young fellow was soon in hospital, stomach pumped and alive. The next day was a Saturday. We'd prepared a family picnic and were just getting into the car to set off when the same young man arrived, released from hospital and desperate to talk. We had no choice. His need was greater than ours. The picnic was off. Being a minister in a village is no sinecure. It's one of the struggles, as well as its greatest joy, that the minister is so well known and is called on to help so many people. Hard work, but deeply satisfying.

From time to time I would get letters from colleagues and friends I'd known in Brazil. I'm sad to say that I sometimes put them on one side "to read when I have time". My new world was requiring a hundred per cent effort. I couldn't handle them both at the same time. I'd still sometimes think of Sheila and the Rikbaktsa people and try to pray for them, but I didn't have anyone to talk to about it. Until Joyce Odell came. When I'd been in Fleckney about three years, Joyce and her husband Richard came to the area for some months. Joyce had been a single-woman missionary in Nepal and had married Richard, who'd been an aid worker in an agricultural project in the same area of Nepal. Now they were back in the UK with baby Ruth, and Richard was working temporarily as a farm manager on a farm near Fleckney, while he waited to do missionary training himself. More than once, Joyce pushed Ruth's pram into Fleckney and came to do some ironing for me or just to talk. How we talked! Here was someone who was actually interested in my life before I was married, asked questions about Brazil, how God had led me to leave it, plus all sorts of things I hardly ever spoke about nowadays. That was a truly healing friendship.

And then something else happened, something that would change the family dynamics for all of us, something that required my coming off anti-depressants – we realised that I was pregnant.

Fleckney Baptist Church

CHAPTER SIXTEEN

The Family Increases

1979 - 1982

The boys were the first people we told that I was pregnant. By the time the baby was born, Jon would be fourteen and Andy and Tim would be ten, old enough not to feel threatened by the arrival of a new baby in the family. Jon was even quite chuffed about it.

I did a bit of supply teaching at Kibworth High School, his school in the village next to ours, and one of his friends asked him, "Is your mum going to have a baby?"

Jon was quite pleased to tell us that he'd replied, "No, she's going to have an elephant!"

All the boys were interested to see some pictures we'd found of a foetus at different stages of development. We consulted these from time to time as the months went on to see "what our baby is looking like now".

When we told our wider family and the church, most people were quite surprised. I suppose it is a bit unusual to be having a first baby at the age of forty-three! But I was overjoyed. Even realising that people thought it odd didn't spoil my enjoyment. When I went to have a check-up at the maternity hospital in Leicester, I looked round the waiting area full of mums-to-be to see if there was anyone anything like my age. There was, so I went and sat with her and got chatting, only to discover that she was there with her daughter who was about to produce the first grandchild! Later, when I went into one of the cubicles to be examined, an Australian doctor put his head round the curtain, took one look at me and said to the nurse, "We've got a right spring chicken here!"

I laughed and said, "That's not very polite."

He said everyone else on the bed that afternoon had been about sixteen! I didn't feel in the least insulted. Nothing could dampen the joy that I was actually going to have a baby.

Because I was older than most, I was given what seemed to be a whole battery of tests. One test that I was offered was an amniocentesis, a test to take off some amniotic fluid to check whether the baby has Down's syndrome or not. We were told that there was a slight possibility that amniocentesis could cause the baby to abort and we made a definite decision to refuse this test. The doctor we told of our decision found it incredible, especially when we explained that even if our baby had a disability, we would not terminate the pregnancy. To him it seemed crazy. To us it was the logical outcome of believing that our baby was a gift to us from God.

The awareness that because of my age, there was a higher chance of his having Down's syndrome remained in my mind. When, at last, Pete was born and was taken from the ward one afternoon to be looked over by the paediatrician, I double-checked with the nurse who brought him back. "He is quite normal, is he? No sign of Down's syndrome?"

"What do you mean?" she retorted. "Can't you see he's perfect?"

And I was reassured, in fact reassured to the extent that I felt quite sorry for the other mums in the ward. It must be hard for them, I found myself thinking, to see that their babies were not nearly as wonderful as mine!

When he was two days old, Philip brought the three boys in to see their little brother. At the end of the hour, when everyone left, Andy reappeared in the doorway to say, "Bye, Pete!" – a clear recognition, I thought, that this little scrap of humanity was accepted as one of the lads! They did accept him. Jon has always been good with babies and tiny children, very caring and protective. Andy and Tim, at ten years old, were proud to push their little brother's buggy round the village.

Philip found that, due to the generous handing on of baby clothes and equipment from other families in the church, this baby was costing us next to nothing – except for lack of sleep at night! And I, in the early months at least, stepped back from any responsibilities in the church, and enjoyed focussing on things at home. It was summer time, the sun shone, Pete slept in his pram in the garden and, for once in our lives, the garden was well kept and weed free! Philip has always enjoyed growing some vegetables, planting onion sets and putting up the sticks for runner beans. He's also great at keeping the grass cut. The rest of it, the borders and pots, are my responsibility. And those are the parts of the garden that are usually most neglected. I just am not good at anything requiring regular routine work. But that year the weather was right, I had more time at home, and the place, for once, looked good.

Friends from New Guinea came to visit. Margaret had been a fellow student at BBI, and had shared that little attic bedroom with me fifteen years earlier. In the meantime, she'd worked with Wycliffe Bible Translators in New Guinea, and had married a widower there, an American dentist called Jim. We had so much to talk about. Margaret and I shared a dislike of the routine of housework and in that context I said, "But there's always the danger of slipping into squalor."

She reassured me, "No, it's not squalor when you plant a lovely clematis by your front door!"

That made me feel a little better about my shortcomings.

I was shocked to see Jim feeding bits of cake to Pete, who was then about three or four months old, fed entirely on mother's milk and already showing signs of having inherited my weight gene. More of a Botticelli than a Lowry, you could say. Jim's excuse made us all laugh: "I thought I'd help to fill out his hollow cheeks!"

When Pete was a toddler, we had another increase in the family, a young man called Dave. He came to us because he'd been working temporarily at Torch Trust, a charity for the blind in another Leicestershire village, and had disgraced himself there by getting into a fight. He was asked to leave, had nowhere to go, and ended up coming to us. We never knew his whole story, though someone told us that he had been a hit man in a city in the north of England. But a dramatic change had occurred in his life.

He told us that he was playing his guitar one day, busking on the streets of Bradford, when a young man came up to him and told him that God loves him.

"Get lost," Dave said, "before I punch you in the face."

The young man did leave, but returned the next day with the same message. This time Dave did punch him, hard. The following day, with a bruised face, the man was back again.

"What is it with you?" Dave asked. "What do I have to do to get you off my back?"

"I'm inviting you to come with me to the cathedral."

And Dave went – anything to get rid of this persistent young idiot! He also thought it could be a laugh. In the middle of the service, when everything was at its most solemn, he planned to get to his feet and start shouting and swearing. They certainly wouldn't invite him again if he caused a massive disturbance! A service had already started when they arrived. They went in quietly and sat down. Everything was peaceful and well ordered. Dave was chuckling inwardly about the havoc he was going to cause. He waited a few minutes, then thought, *"Now!"*

But he couldn't do it. Something was pinning him to his seat. Something much stronger than he was. He sat until the end of the service, terrified. When it was over, the young man sitting beside him was concerned.

"Something wrong?" he asked, and Dave, with a few expletives, told him he was paralysed, he could not move.

One of the cathedral staff came and prayed with him and the paralysis went. Physically he was back to normal, but inwardly he was changed. He had had a personal encounter with Almighty God. From then on he had thought of himself as a Christian and had mingled with Christians all over the country. Now he was with us.

In some ways his being there was a good thing for us. He taught Tim to play the guitar, and that has been a lifetime joy for Tim. Dave taught me something too. In his travels, he had once worked in the kitchen of a hotel in Cornwall, and he gave me some tips about making food tasty and interesting.

But there were things we found difficult. I think Jon found it hard that he was no longer the eldest "child" and he and Dave would sometimes argue. One of those arguments gave me a memory to treasure.

I was making scrambled eggs for tea and said, "I'll put some bits of bacon in it" – and was surprised at the disgusted reaction of Dave.

It turned out that he thought of scrambled eggs as being a dessert, sweet like an egg custard. But Jon leapt to my defence.

"Don't be daft, Dave. Bacon and eggs go together great."

It touched my heart that Jon should be taking my side when he'd had such difficulty accepting me.

Philip found it difficult to have another drain on our meagre finances. It wasn't just another mouth to feed. It was that Dave had become used to the way that Christians hold their possessions lightly, and was very happy to make use of anything we had. There were two single inflatable mattresses that we used for camping holidays and for the boys to sleep on when relatives came to stay; they met their demise when Dave used them one summer's day as rafts on Saddington Reservoir! Philip lent Dave his motorbike for a trip down to Cornwall and it was driven at such breakneck speed all the way that its engine never recovered. We tried not to complain. We tried to keep on loving and praying and believing that God was working in his life as he is in us all. None of us is a finished product while we are down here.

One area that we'd have liked to see a change in Dave was in his attitude to women. Sometimes it amused us. Sometimes it was more serious. In the summer, we took our tents and went off on a camping holiday at a Christian convention. There's a great atmosphere at events like that. People are friendly and courteous and everyone feels very safe. So it was a shock for one young woman, walking quietly through the tents to the toilet block at about 6 am one morning, to hear a piercing wolf-whistle and to see Dave's face leering at her from under the wall of a tent she was passing!

There came a day when I, too, crossed swords with Dave. In those days, there was a widespread fashion for Citizens' Band two-way radios – Dave had one in his room and used it all the time. His "handle" on the airwaves was "the Bishop", and he made no secret of the fact that he was living with a minister's family. One day as I was passing his bedroom door, I heard such a bawdy conversation that I burst in on him in the middle of his transmission and said, "Dave, no way are you going to broadcast that sort of rubbish from our house!" He was shocked into silence seeing me in a tougher mode than usual.

As the months went on, he decided that he wanted to go on a mission to another church and we encouraged him to apply. It would be good for him, we thought, to be part of a team of young Christians and to use his undoubted musical skills. He was accepted and duly went off to East Anglia. A couple of weeks later we had a phone call from

Dave's team leader who told us a sad story. Dave had been billeted with a family who were comfortably off and had some valuable jewellery. One day they discovered that some pieces of jewellery were missing, and it turned out that Dave had taken them and sold them to a pawnbroker. His team leader had decided that he couldn't remain on the team and was sending him home to us. Quite early the next morning Dave arrived home. He began his explanation of why he was back earlier than expected. He hadn't enjoyed it, hadn't got on well with the rest of the team, had decided to quit and come home.

"Dave," Philip said, "we've already had a phone call from your team leader. He told us what happened."

"Oh, we'll talk later," said Dave. "I've just got to go down to the village for some cigarettes." And that was the last we saw of him for a couple of years. Losing Dave in that way made us feel a sense of loss and of failure. He had so much potential for good, and we'd not been able to help him realise it.

He had done us good though. We had learned that our home isn't just ours. It's to be used, like everything we have, for others, for whomever God sends, at whatever cost. Dave was the first of many men, women and young people who have shared our home for shorter or longer periods of time. Sometimes it's been a struggle, sometimes a delight, but we have never looked back and regretted welcoming someone. It feels like a privilege to have a home to share.

Shortly after Dave left, we nearly left Fleckney ourselves.

Family group

CHAPTER SEVENTEEN

The Boys are Growing Up

1982 - 1985

Philip had begun to feel unsettled in the church and we'd been thinking that if we were going to make a change, the best time to do it would be in the summer of 1983. Jon would be nearly eighteen then and would have finished his course at the catering college in Leicester. Andy and Tim would be fourteen, about to embark on their GCSE syllabus. And Pete would be four. So, for all of them it would be a reasonable time for a change. Whenever Philip or I had invitations to speak at churches that autumn, we said that we were really sorry but we were not free on that date, but no-one except the two of us and Eric, our faithful church secretary, knew what we were thinking.

We began to look into the possibility of Philip working as a representative of an overseas mission – he had recently been to Nigeria to visit his brother, and that had reawakened his interest in Africa, where he had lived as a boy. An opening arose, we went for interview, and Philip was offered the job. We had to give a definite yes or no by a certain Thursday when the mission were due to have a committee meeting. On the Monday evening, Philip told our church elders in confidence, and asked them to pray for God to bring about whatever he wanted. On the Tuesday evening, he told the deacons – the rest of the church leadership. On the Wednesday, Philip and I agreed not to talk any more about it, but that each of us would pray separately and trust God to show us both what he wanted us to do. As the day went on, I became more and more certain that it would be the wrong move for us. At our interview, the mission leaders had been somewhat concerned about what they would have called our "charismatic tendencies". Sadly, in those days, the work of the Holy Spirit in people's lives had become a divisive issue. Philip and I were grateful for any experience of the Spirit's help and empowering and then, as now, would have been eager for more evidence of the work of God's Spirit in our lives. This had made the committee a bit wary of us, even though they had, in the end, decided to offer Philip the job. Thinking about it during that day of decision, I really did not want Philip to work in that atmosphere of wariness. But how was he feeling?

We had arranged to talk on Wednesday afternoon before the boys came in from school. It was a wonderful moment. Philip, after feeling unsettled and discouraged for several months, had had a total change of heart. He was now refreshed and positive, sure that God had given him a fresh call to continue as pastor in that church and that village.

I don't think we even told the boys that we had so nearly left. Fleckney had been their home since they were tiny and they were surrounded there with friends and people who cared about them.

The twins were not popular with everyone, however. One day, when they were about twelve, they arrived home off the school bus quiet and unhappy. At first, when I asked them what the matter was, they didn't want to tell me. They were afraid I'd go and confront the person responsible and make matters worse! It turned out that there had been some bullying on the bus. A bigger boy had taken one of their school bags and had used it as a weapon to batter them. We knew him and his family. If there was ever a fight outside the village pub, this boy's dad would be at the heart of it. The way his son had been behaving on the bus would not have seemed abnormal to that family. I told Andy and Tim what Jesus says about our attitude to people who treat us badly: "Pray for those who persecute you." So we did. We prayed for the boy and for his family.

As we came to the "Amen", Andy looked up and said, "I feel different now. I'm not afraid of him anymore. In fact, I feel sorry for him."

How wise of Jesus! He uses our prayers not only to help the people we pray for, but to help us too.

As they grew up, the twins, though identical in appearance, were emerging as very different characters. Andy was a quiet lad, painstaking and thorough. He was a committed Christian and, when he was fifteen, was already starting up and running a small Christian Union at school. He was the leader of the twins, the one who organised a tidy up of their bedroom from time to time, the one who bought birthday cards and put them in Tim's hand to sign. Tim was a good follower, not quick to make decisions himself, but cheerfully fitting in with whatever was planned. He was musical, very skilled on his guitar, and chatty and popular amongst his friends. They had different hobbies too. Tim's guitar was important to him, and he was still interested in bird watching. Andy had a drum kit, and was developing an interest in butterflies. They both loved Technical Lego and computers – we'd managed to buy a second-hand computer for their bedroom. By now, I had a regular job – teaching RE part-time at Kibworth High School – so finances weren't quite as tight as they had been, but we still could not afford the foreign school trips and the up-to-the-minute clothing and electronic things that most teenagers seemed to have.

Once I said to them, "I'm so sorry, boys, that we can't give you all the stuff that some of your friends have."

Andy was indignant. "Mum, just stand in our bedroom doorway and look around. We've got everything we need."

They were teenagers though; they were not perfect. All the boys had their grumpy moments, their inconsiderate moments – such as playing loud music. I chuckled one day at the response of some of our neighbours to the volume of music. It was a hot day and the windows were wide open. I was in the garden hanging out the washing, but aware that Abba was coming out loud and clear from one of the bedroom windows. Two elderly ladies from a rather strict church nearby – not quite as restrictive as the Exclusive Brethren had been, but something of the same flavour – were walking up the street at the side of our house, and I heard one say to the other in disgusted tones, "And they call themselves Christians!"

It hadn't been easy for the boys, growing up in a village where their father was the local minister. Another young boy had once said to Jon, "Why doesn't your father have a proper job?" And somehow it doesn't do anything for your street cred as a teenager when your father is a minister and your mother teaches RE!

We were out for a walk one Sunday afternoon, coming across the fields from the canal, when a cheeky young lad called out, "You're just a load of God-bods!"

The boys said, "Ignore him, Mum!"

But no, I was marching over to the boy and his friends, smiling at them and saying, "I know that you meant to insult us but, actually, I'm very glad that I'm a follower of Jesus. And I wish you were one too!"

Something similar happened on the school bus when the twins were about fifteen. As everybody was getting on the bus, one young fellow said, "No room at the back of the bus. It's that God-bod in my seat there."

Andy and Tim and a good half-dozen of their friends from the church youth group all got to their feet and said together as if they'd been practising it, "Yer mean me?"

Everybody laughed and the moment was defused.

I've said a lot about the twins, but how about Jon? He didn't have a twin. There weren't so many of his age group in the church at that time. And he'd got a stepmother he struggled to relate to. His teenage years were a lonely time.

And Pete? How had he fared in these years while his big brothers were growing up? Bless them, they had continued to be patient and loving towards him as he changed from a cuddly baby into a toddler who knew how to turn the television off even in the middle of their favourite programmes, and then into someone who invaded their bedrooms until we put little bolts on their doors, high up, out of the reach of a four-year-old. His playschool leader said once that she thought he was shy because he would stand uncertainly at the edge of the crowd. But I thought that he was probably working out how he could get in there and take charge – I felt that, if anything, he was too sure of himself. By the time he started school, he was already reading, quite confident and with several good friends.

We must have seemed quite a happy family. And yes, God had been incredibly good to us, and had brought us through some very difficult times. But there was another one ahead, perhaps the hardest one of all.

CHAPTER EIGHTEEN

Our Saddest Time of All

1985

It was Easter 1985. Easter Sunday is always a special day, but it was made extra special for me that year because we had a Brazilian family staying in the village. The husband, a minister, had come to England to do further studies in Theology, but before he started studying, he needed to improve his English. He had had a term with his family at one of the Selly Oak colleges in Birmingham, working on English, and now, for a break at Easter, they had come to stay in Fleckney. On the Sunday I had the joy of interpreting for him when he gave a brief message in Portuguese at church – it was a rare treat for me to hear Portuguese, eleven years after coming home from Brazil.

On Easter Monday they came to lunch with us and then Philip, Pete and I went for a walk with them to Foxton Locks on the Grand Union Canal. When we returned to the village, they decided to go back to the house where they were staying. We planned to see them again the next day. At home Andy was feeling very cheerful. He'd spent the afternoon practising on his drums, had recorded himself and was quite impressed with his progress. He wanted us to have a quick tea; then, when a friend arrived to give us all a haircut, Andy wanted to be first because he was meeting his girlfriend Rachel that evening. So, we got ourselves organised, had tea, Audrey arrived and cut Andy's hair, and then continued to work her way one by one through the family. When Tim's was done, he went upstairs to the twins' bedroom. He heard a strange squeal there, and thought it must be Andy and Pete playing, but no, Pete was downstairs. In their bedroom, Andy was lying still on the floor.

Tim came down to Philip, busy as usual with the washing-up, and told him that there was something wrong with Andy. Something *was* wrong – *very* wrong. Andy had been electrocuted. Philip phoned a friend, Helen, a nurse who lived just up the road, and she came immediately and began artificial respiration. Other phone calls brought an ambulance and our local doctor, but all to no avail. Andy was dead.

It turned out that he had taken a shower, come back into the bedroom still damp, fallen over a metal heater and landed with his hand on an old hairdryer motor that the boys used to power their Technical Lego models. And the motor was still plugged in – we could see the burn from the motor on his hand.

News of his death was round the village in no time. Jon ran across to tell Rachel, Andy's girlfriend. Helen phoned our church members. The house became full of shocked people wanting to be with us in our grief, wanting to pray, wanting to hug us, wanting to understand. The electricity board sent a team to check that the house was safe. I offered them a cup of tea but they embarrassedly refused; it must have been so hard for them having to do their work in a house full of shock and pain. The undertaker came and took Andy's body away.

Pete was five now and it was past his bedtime. I put him to bed, but he couldn't sleep and called me back.

"Mummy, why did Jesus let Andy die?"

"I don't know. But we don't need to know. Jesus knows."

"Oh, that's all right then. Jesus will be explaining to Andy, won't he?"

That comment did me so much good. In my mind now, Andy wasn't a dead body lying on the bedroom floor. He was a living boy walking along beside Jesus and getting his questions answered.

The day before, we had sung a song joyfully asserting that we can face the future without fear because Jesus is alive. When we sang it on Sunday, we hadn't known what the Monday would bring. But we were to sing the same song again with heartache, although just as much certainty, at Andy's funeral.

There were nights and days to be got through before the funeral. That first night we made up a bed for Tim on the living-room floor – we didn't want him to sleep alone in the room where his twin had just died. But Tim didn't sleep much that night and nor did any of us. Night seems to be the time when our minds try to process the things that have happened during the day. Early in the morning, Philip and I went down to make a cup of tea, found Tim awake, and sat on his bed drinking tea and talking. Around seven o'clock there was a knock at the front door and there was our friend, the Brazilian pastor. He had come round to read the Bible and pray with us. How lovely was that – this week of all weeks there was another pastor in the village, eager to help us!

Several of the church asked what they could do to help, and we asked some of them to look after the Brazilians and take them out for a day, so that their holiday wouldn't be spoilt by our being out of action. People made a rota and did that. Helen, the nurse, had noticed that I had a basket of wet laundry waiting. In that day, busy with visitors, I hadn't had time to dry it – she took it to her house and returned it a couple of days later, not only dried but ironed as well. Others brought us food, a huge ham, a weekly chocolate cake – so many kind and generous gestures. One of Andy's friends, who shared his interest in butterflies, gave us a brimstone butterfly he had caught and mounted. (This lad went home and told his mum that "Philip and Joan both looked ten years older" – I'm sure we felt it!) The bully-boy, who had attacked the twins three or four years before, came to our door. He wanted to say how good Andy had been to him – Andy had lent him his hi-hat when he needed one for his drum kit. The undertaker came to talk to us and told us he was not going to charge us anything for the funeral. A decorator friend came and, without any charge, decorated Tim's bedroom to give him a fresh start. Scores of people sent us cards and letters. Andy's RE teacher wrote, "He had the makings of a man of God." The vicar of Fleckney Parish Church cut short a holiday to be there at the funeral. A neighbour came to the door saying, "I don't know why I've come. I've no idea what to say." And we just hugged one another and cried. She came in and we sat by the fire with mugs of tea remembering and crying. I look back on that as being the most helpful of all visits.

The least helpful was one of our own church members who said angrily, "I can't understand why God has done this to Philip and you."

That hurt me deeply. It sounded as if God was distant somewhere, causing nasty things to happen to people. I didn't feel like that. I felt as if he was with us, weeping with us, understanding and sharing our pain. Another church member said something strange, no doubt thinking of me as a step-parent. "I've been wondering how you've been feeling," she said, "because in a way you're not involved, are you?" Perhaps she was right that if I'd been Andy's biological mother, I would have felt an even deeper pain. But you don't look after a child for ten years and feel "not involved".

These people came to our house. For us to leave the house was somehow harder. Three days after Andy's death would have been his sixteenth birthday. Now Tim, for the first time, would have a birthday alone. The day before, Pete and I went down the village to buy cards for Tim. Just walking to the shop and going through the door seemed a huge effort of willpower. Actually making a choice and deciding what card to buy took all the strength I had. I was so glad that five-year-old Pete was there, looking for his own card, wanting me to confirm that Tim would like the one he'd chosen. The shopkeeper didn't speak about Andy, but there hung unspoken sympathy in the air between us. I should have said something to make it easier for him.

One day I made that first move. A neighbour from a few doors away whom we knew only slightly was passing our house as I was speaking to someone at the front door. The neighbour was looking at me as he went by, looking and looking. I realised he wanted to say something, but didn't know how. So I excused myself for a moment from the person at the door and went out to the neighbour. "Thank you," I said. "You were looking so sympathetic." And I gave him a hug. They moved house a few days later, and their removal van was stolen with all their possessions inside it. They wrote to us to say that their loss of furniture, children's toys, books and photos would have been much more devastating if they hadn't been comparing it with our loss of a son.

Our next hurdle was preparing for the funeral. We planned it as a family. Each of us chose a hymn or a piece of music to listen to, and we put together an order of service leaflet with pictures of drums, computers and butterflies around Andy's photo on the front. This was a teenager's funeral – we didn't want it to be the same as a funeral for an elderly person. Philip decided to ask Mike Elcome and Bruce Stokes, ministers from other Baptist churches in South Leicestershire, to take the service between them. They agreed, but naturally felt it a daunting task. They came over to talk to us about it one morning. I think it was Bruce who was going to preach. He said that he'd been praying about it but had felt no guidance about what to say, so we found Andy's bible to see if that gave us any clues – anything underlined or highlighted to show that it had been special to him. Folded in the pages of the bible was a question sheet that the youth leader had given the boys one Sunday morning some months before. It included the question, "If you died tonight and God said, 'Why should I let you into my heaven?' what would you say?" Andy had written, "Because Jesus died for me, and I'm trying to live for him." That touched all our hearts and helped Bruce with his sermon.

The ladies of the church suggested that we arrange the funeral for early afternoon so that there would be no need of a big meal afterwards, and said they would all make cakes and serve tea to everyone who came. So that's what we did. We put on a cold lunch at home beforehand, using that huge ham we'd been given, and relatives and friends from afar came there first. As I was preparing the meal, who should appear at the front door but Dave, the young man who had once lived with us but disappeared in a hurry a couple of years before. I was pleased to see him, gave him a kiss and asked him in.

"No thanks," he said, "but I heard of Andy's death and wanted to come to the funeral. The only thing is, I haven't enough money for the petrol for the journey back..."

So, we handed over a fiver and hoped that would be a help.

"And can I take Tim back with me for a while?"

"I don't think that's going to work out – sorry. He has his GCSE exams in a few weeks. Thanks for inviting him all the same. You sure you can't come in for lunch? Bless you for coming. We'll see you later."

We heard afterwards that he'd been to the doors of several Christian homes in the village, mentioned his need for petrol, and must have gone away with a fair few five and ten pound notes. What an enigma he was!

Other people arrived. My parents weren't able to come because my dad was by now seriously incapacitated with Parkinson's disease. We'd been able to send the order of service to them before the day, so they could share in the funeral that way, and Philip and I were going to go up and see them the following week, so they could see for themselves that we were all right. But Bryan and Janet were there, as was Hilary (Harold was ill, sadly), and some of Ann's relatives and some of Philip's. It was quite a crowd, but we all helped ourselves to food in the kitchen and milled around the house and garden eating and chatting.

Then down to church. The little church was packed to the rafters, and the hall (which was normally used for the toddler group and youth activities) was filled with every chair that could be found and the sound was piped through to the crowd there. Someone said to us afterwards that the whole village seemed to come to a standstill and to share in mourning. We sat on the front row, Pete first, then me, then Tim in the middle because his loss was the greatest of all, then Philip and Jon. Crowds of young people were there and one of Andy's friends had a drum kit set up in the balcony to join in with the organ for the more rousing hymns, things like:

Thine be the glory, risen conquering Son.
Endless is the victory Thou o'er death hast won.

Some days later, going to the shops, I met a mum from the village who was not a person of faith herself, even though she'd been brought up in a believing family. I'd seen her at the funeral and took the opportunity now of thanking her for coming. "It was a strange experience," she said. "For a few minutes, I actually believed." I don't know where she is now but as I write this, I find myself praying that those few minutes have grown into a lasting faith.

After the service in the church we invited anyone who wished to, to come with us to the cemetery in Wigston, about five miles away. Dozens of people came and, after the interment, someone spontaneously began to sing again and we all joined in:

Thine be the glory, risen conquering Son.

I didn't feel able to talk to people anymore and walked back to the car, followed by our kind undertaker. But then I had to say to him, "Oh, I'm sorry. I've got to go back after all. I've not given his little girlfriend a hug." He was such a very kind friend. When we all got back to the cars, he asked young Pete to sit in the front seat next to him and hold the top hat! And as we were driving solemnly up a hill on the way back to Fleckney, he asked our permission to stop the car for a minute, while he ran back down the hill to pick up a hubcap that had fallen off the limo and gone bowling down the hill behind us! We had a little chuckle over that.

Andy was buried in the grave where his mother had been placed eleven years before. There was space on the gravestone for another inscription, but we didn't have that done straight away. Philip wanted to have time to think and get the words just right. In the end, he adapted some words from the Psalms. Engraved at the base of the headstone now is:

and her son
Andrew Philip Kearney
died 8 April 1985, aged 15

"Full of joy in the presence of Jesus"

Some weeks later, Pete came home from Sunday School very excited. For the first time he had heard the story of Jesus raising a dead girl back to life.

"Do you think Jesus could bring Andy back, Mum?" he wanted to know.

I was putting pans on the stove for lunch, so could take a quick moment to pray before I looked at him with my answer.

"Yes, Jesus certainly could," I said, "but the problem is, I'm not sure whether Andy would want to come back now. He's having such a lovely time in heaven with Jesus."

He is.

CHAPTER NINETEEN

Keeping Going

1985 - 1992

How were those of us still on earth coping with Andy's death? I went back to school a few days late after the start of the summer term. Each class I taught in my first week back, I took some minutes at the start of the lesson to talk about Andy's death. I taught at the middle school of a three-tier system. The twins by that time had moved to the upper school in Market Harborough, ten miles away. For that reason, not all the children would have known him personally, even if they all knew the fact that he had died. I told them how it had happened and gave them the opportunity to ask questions. Unusually, in my classes, they were profoundly quiet and respectful. Years later, one boy said to his mother, "I'll never forget how Mrs Kearney talked to us when her son had died." There seems to be a breaking down of generational barriers when someone of an older generation shares something painful with younger ones. I got through it by being factual and quietly controlled.

The only time I nearly broke down at school was in the staff room one break. That day, Tim had left for the school bus with a GCSE exam looming over him. I had watched his back as he went down the path, alone, looking somehow less tall than usual, seeming utterly desolate. At break that morning, as we sipped our coffee, a friend said, "How's

Tim doing?" I couldn't put into words how he must be feeling. I was too choked even to try.

For Tim, the adjustment to being without Andy took a very long time. Needing someone to make decisions led him over the years to some girlfriends who were bossy and demanding – not at all the sort of girl we longed to see him with. As we'd expected, his exam results that year reflected the emotional turmoil he was in, so he went into the sixth form for a year to resit them before going on to an engineering apprenticeship. He still found great enjoyment in his music and was part of a little group called "Firm Promise" that played in our church and some other churches around the area.

For Jon, the death of Andy was a turning point. For years he had shut away his memories of Ann. But now death became an okay thing to talk about. He chose a hymn that he remembered being sung at his Mum's funeral for us to sing at Andy's funeral. He went frequently up to Helen's house to ask questions about Ann's illness. One night we heard him crying in bed and Philip went through and had a father-and-son heart-to-heart that they had not been able to achieve before. A buried anguish was surfacing and finding some healing.

Pete seemed to cope more easily. Yes, he did miss Andy, but he was too young to know how rare and shocking the death of a teenager is. A young child seems to take events on board more calmly, as if recognising, "Oh, so that's one of the things that happens in life, is it?" One day he told us that the head teacher had brought the school doctor to see him, and they'd asked him about Andy. I don't know why or what they'd talked about, but he seemed unfazed by it.

And Philip? A friend in the village, not yet a convinced Christian at the time, said to his wife, "Philip will never preach again now. Only in his mid-forties and he's already buried a wife and a young son." But Philip did continue to preach, and to work, and to care for the lonely and sad in the village. In fact, in some ways his faith was stronger. The fact that our faith had survived a major blow made us realise more than ever that it is real. God was seeing us through. He was still there.

We were so very glad that we had not moved from Fleckney a couple of years before. It seemed important to be surrounded by a caring village where people knew us and had known Andy. Many people in the village were thinking about their own lives. Usually in youth or middle-age we feel eternal – death is something that happens to old people! But when a boy dies suddenly and unexpectedly, everyone feels less secure. Around that time, a team of people from our church were visiting interested people in Fleckney to talk about what the Bible teaches and that particular week they had arranged to visit Sue, who wanted to know what her boys were being taught in the youth club. As they arrived, she immediately said, "I'm so glad you're here. Since I heard of Andrew Kearney's death I've not been able to sleep. What if it had been me?" They were able to explain to her that there is hope for us all. Not because we're perfect – nobody is. But because Jesus has died for us, God is more than happy to forgive us, give us a clean slate and welcome us – when our time comes – into his heaven. Sue grasped it straight away, prayed her own prayer, saying sorry for the years she had ignored God and thanking him for Jesus. And then she began to feel at peace. She became a much-appreciated part of the church after that.

She also became my helper at home. Now that I was teaching about half-time at school, we could afford to pay someone to clean for me and, as she came one of the days when I was at home, we did a bit of chatting as well as cleaning and became good friends.

Losing Andy had changed me. At home, I was more accepting of the boys than I had ever been, just thankful to have them still. And at Easter the next year, when Jon was twenty, something happened that was to give our relationship a whole new beginning.

You may remember Richard and Joyce Odell. They had come from Nepal and spent some months in Fleckney during my early years there. Since then, our village had been their base in the UK when they came back on home-leave from Nepal. This time, Richard had come by himself. He had damaged his knee in a motorbike accident, and had returned on crutches to have treatment for it, leaving Joyce and the children in Pokhara, Nepal. He was to be in Fleckney over the Easter weekend, so Philip invited him to lead the Maundy Thursday service. Our custom was to have a communion service sitting round in a circle, remembering how Jesus had a meal with his disciples the evening before he was executed, and how he'd asked them to remember him when they ate bread and drank wine together. There was another event during that last evening of the life of Jesus on earth: Jesus took a bowl of water and, doing the work a servant would usually do in those days, washed his disciples' feet. Richard suggested that we do the same thing. It involved a bit of planning. People brought washing-up bowls and towels and there was a boiler of warm water. At one stage in the evening, Richard invited us to get a bowl of water and wash the feet of someone else in the group. The first person to move was a young man of whom one of the older men had been very critical. The young man took a bowl of water, knelt at the feet of the one who had been so hard on him, and gently washed his feet. It was tremendously moving. Then I took a bowl and went to a brave young woman whose life was one of cheerful dedication and service to others. I wanted her to know how much her self-sacrifice was treasured by Jesus. All around us people were washing one another's feet, praying together, crying together. An amazing evening! But most precious of all to me was that Jon brought a bowl over and washed my feet. We hugged one another, said sorry, and shed a few tears. It was a turning point, where our mutual love of Jesus became something that generated a love and understanding between us that had not seemed possible before.

Jon had finished his training at catering college and could have become a chef, but realised that chefs generally work evenings and at weekends – the very times when most church activities take place. For that reason, he chose not to be a chef, and had a number of jobs in fast-food outlets, working at different times for Domino's Pizzas and Wimpy. Sometimes his work took him to different parts of the country, which was sad for us at home. But it was great to have a grown-up son. One time when he came home, he put mugs of tea in Philip's hand and mine and sat us down for a serious discussion about a decision he had to make. We appreciated that very much.

Tim was living at home and training as an engineering apprentice. He once moved out for a few months to share a house in the village with some mates, but it all proved more expensive than they'd expected and he soon moved home again. We'd missed him and were glad he was back. He was not finding it easy to relate to God at this stage of his life. Like many children of Christian parents, he seemed to feel that he'd missed out on some of the fun his mates were having, and he needed to try out for himself what life had to offer.

One Christmas Eve, I was at home babysitting Pete, Philip was at the midnight Christmas Eve service, and Tim came in from the pub feeling very ill. He managed to get upstairs to the bathroom to be sick and I followed him, offering what sympathy and help I could.

At one moment I asked him, “Whatever made you drink so much, Tim?”

“I wanted to celebrate.”

“Oh dear, it doesn’t look a lot of fun.”

It didn’t, and my heart was wrung for him in his lonely, desperate attempt to make life happy again. By the time Philip came in, Tim was in bed sleeping it off, and I didn’t say anything to Philip about it until late the next day.

Through those years the thing that helped Tim the most was probably his music. He and some friends started a band called MHGBU, short for “My Head’s Going to Blow Up”, which was involved in gigs in venues all over the East Midlands and as far afield as York in the north and Portsmouth in the South. As time went on, Tim was the only one in the group in employment. He provided the van to carry them and their equipment, so worked hard at setting up, playing and packing away. He then drove home late at night, unloaded and somehow managed to be up early in the morning to be at work for 7.30 am. Life was very full and busy, and that helped.

We all kept very busy. I’ve recently been looking through some of Philip’s old diaries from those days and am amazed how much we managed to pack into life. As well as our responsibilities at home and in the church, we both spoke fairly frequently at other churches, and were used from time to time for “Thought for the Day” and other religious broadcasting on BBC Radio Leicester. One time, Philip did a week’s “Thoughts for the Day” on the theme of death. A neighbour gave him a message from her elderly mum: “Every morning I’ve stood by the radio, with my elbows on the sideboard and my face in my hands, listening to every word. Tell that man that he’s done me a power of good.”

For some years I was busy at school. I was never a brilliant teacher of teenagers – much too soft! One time, trying to get silence to give my carefully prepared lesson, I banged a book on the table. They all stopped their conversations, looked at me and went very quiet. My face was white and unsmiling. They probably assumed it was white with rage, but no. The truth was that I’d stupidly had a finger under the book as it hit the table, and I was white with pain! But of course I couldn’t admit that. I had to seize the moment of quiet and get on with the lesson, pain or not!

It wasn't all bad, though. In the first term for the eleven-year-olds who had just come up to the school, we did a series of lessons that aimed to show that religious belief is rational. It reminded me of my Philosophy of Religion studies years before. We cannot prove with logic that there is a God (but neither can atheists prove that there isn't). We can use various arguments, however, to show that it's quite reasonable to suppose that there is a God – and then, acting on that supposition, taking that step of faith, life can confirm to us that he is real. The books that we used for this part of the course were stimulating and child friendly. I loved it. And so did some of the youngsters. I was hugely encouraged by one bright-eyed young lad as he went out at the end of the lesson: "I thought RE were gonna be dead boring, but it's not, is it?"

Despite such moments, I eventually decided to leave teaching. I just did not have time for the necessary hours of preparation, marking and doing reports. Marking, especially. I would take a pile of exercise books home to be marked, be busy non-stop at home with the demands of the family, answering the phone, talking to people who came to see us, going to one meeting, preparing for another... and would take the books back to school the next day unmarked. I didn't deserve the good salary I was being given. Instead I got a little job as assistant warden in a block of flats for elderly people. It was minimal pay compared with teaching, but a great opportunity to be involved in our village life and make friends with a different group of people. With one woman, I failed. There was one old lady who resented our calling to check on her wellbeing, and was always grumpy. I made it my goal to get her to smile, but sadly never achieved it. Poor old soul!

In those years our little church was becoming something of a centre for Christian counselling. Philip and our dear friend Judith had been away to the Crusade for World Revival (CWR) for some training, and had come back and taught listening skills to a group in the church. Eventually we could afford for me to go and have some training too and I was able to join the counselling team. I felt very privileged and humbled when people came and opened up their hearts and shared their deepest hurts.

One man referred to us by CWR came from some miles away, suffering from depression. He told us his story. He was the youngest child, like me, and had always felt inferior to his brother and sister.

When they were children, his parents had been medical missionaries working at a riverside hospital in a tropical forest somewhere. He and his siblings were away at boarding school in the city. He remembered the excitement of the start of the school holidays, the boat journey along the river to get home, the joy of seeing his parents again. He remembered the pleasures of the holidays, the freedom of going fishing along the river and the moments when the family ate together and talked. And he remembered the pain of standing among the crowd of patients at the hospital and watching his mother, so busy caring for the queue of suffering people that she didn't even seem to see him there. That memory seemed to be at the heart of his sadness, so we stayed with it for a while. We reminded him that Jesus was there too, and he knew just how that little boy was feeling.

I said, "I think Jesus wanted to come and ask you to show him the best places for fishing."

We sat while he thought and imagined that scenario. Then he smiled.

"What's happening?" we asked.

"I caught the first fish, but now Jesus has caught some too, and we're going to take them home and cook them for all the family."

Silence again for a while.

"What's going on now?"

"We're sitting round the table eating the fish. Everyone's happy and talking to Jesus."

"Do you feel pushed out, now that all the others are there?"

"No, because Jesus keeps looking at me and smiling."

More silence for a while. Then he stirred in his seat and seemed to be back in the present again.

"Hold on to that experience," we told him. "It may not have happened physically when you were a little lad. But it's a spiritual reality. Jesus was there. He did care about you, and did totally understand. He did want to spend time with you and share your life and smile at you... He feels the same way about you now."

We moved away not long afterwards and I've no idea what happened to his depression, but that experience must have enriched his life. Sharing it certainly enriched mine.

Moved away? You mean you actually left Fleckney? Yes, we did. Not Jon and Tim. They bought a little house together, just up the road from the manse where they had lived for over twenty years, and carried on with their jobs and their circle of friends. But for Philip, Pete and me, a new adventure was about to begin.

Chapter Twenty

Moving to Nepal

1992 - 1995

A few years before, our friend Eric had generously paid for Philip and me to visit a young missionary couple and their baby in Pakistan, and Richard and Joyce and their children in Nepal. Both families were members of our church and we had prayed for them and sent money regularly for their support. It had been thrilling for us to have the opportunity to actually visit them. At the end of a wonderful month, as the plane lifted out of the haze of the Kathmandu valley to a glorious view of the mountains, we each said to one another that we didn't feel we were saying goodbye to Nepal forever. Obviously we couldn't think of working overseas at that time. We felt that the older boys, although growing up quickly, still needed the security of having us around. But we kept in our hearts the hope that some day we'd have the opportunity of working together as missionaries somewhere in the world.

Then one day in 1991 there was a phone call. The director of the International Nepal Fellowship (INF) was in England briefly, and wanted to get in contact with us because INF were looking for a pastoral couple to support their team of medical missionaries – and Richard and Joyce had mentioned our names as possibly filling the bill. Philip was out, so the director explained to me what the job would involve and then said, "I know you can't make any sort of decision without taking time for discussion and prayer, but could you just give me some idea of your initial reaction?"

That was easy: "Yippee!"

There followed great discussions between Philip and me, talking about the possibility of moving away from the church and from Jon and Tim and our elderly relatives, and discussing Pete's ongoing education at the mission school in Kathmandu.

We didn't tell Pete that it was a strong possibility, but I did sound him out one day. I said, "If God moved us away from Fleckney one day, perhaps even to work in another country, how would you feel about it?"

He replied, "I wouldn't want to go, but if God wanted us to, I suppose we'd have to."

We could sympathise. Fleckney had been his home all his life. Philip and I were both eager to go, but prayed that God would stop us in our tracks if it wasn't part of his plan.

Then came the application papers – all those pages to fill in once again – informal chats with some INFers on home leave and a formal interview at the INF office in Birmingham. The people at the office knew me fairly well – for some years I'd been on the committee interviewing new candidates – but they didn't know Philip, and there were things about me that they hadn't been aware of before.

One of the questions on the papers was, "Which Christian book, apart from the Bible, has influenced you the most?" and I had chosen "Celebration of Discipline" by Richard Foster.

"Why that book?" they asked.

And I had to say, "Because I need it! By nature I'm extremely undisciplined – eat too much, hate doing boring routine jobs..."

They laughed, but it's true – and not really a laughing matter.

They accepted us all the same. Suddenly our lives were going to have a major upheaval. How was it all going to work out? When we told Pete, he was devastated. He was twelve, with many friends in the village and in the church, comfortable at the high school where I used to teach, and able to get by at school with minimal effort. In the months before we left for Nepal, I saw that he was putting on weight and I discovered that his school dinner money was being spent on visits to the sweet shop every day. Oh dear, was it comfort-eating to help him cope with the changes ahead? It's sad seeing your own sins reappearing in the next generation.

Jon and Tim were preparing in a mature way for being without us. With the help of good friends, they were able to go to London and bid at an auction there for a repossessed house in Fleckney. There was a mistake in the catalogue, which showed the wrong picture beside the details of the house, a much less-attractive picture, and this may have contributed to the fact that they were able to get the house at less than its market value. They took out a mortgage together. That gave them a start in the housing market that has been a blessing in subsequent years.

Our elderly relatives, thankfully, were well cared for. My father had passed away by that time, and after a stroke, my mother was in a nursing home, but Hilary lived nearby and was doing a sterling job of visiting Mum every day. Philip's father had died, too, but his mother was in a granny flat next to his brother's home. Ann's mother had also died, but the children's granddad was in sheltered housing owned by his church, and Jon popped in frequently and took on the responsibility of being next of kin for him and for an ageing great aunt. We were somewhat embarrassed that we could do so little to help, but were deeply thankful for each of those who had cheerfully accepted these responsibilities, and we realised gratefully that this now freed us to go overseas again.

For the church at Fleckney, it was going to be a big adjustment after having Philip as their minister for over twenty years. One person said, though, "If we have to lose our minister, there couldn't be a better way than for God to have called him to missionary work." And they chose as their new pastor a young man who had grown up in the village and who had worked in Pakistan for a time – the very one whom Philip and I had visited there three or four years before.

We had to sort out our possessions: things to take with us, things to get rid of, and things to leave at the boys' new house. Some of the furniture and kitchen stuff they could make use of and some things they stored for us in their little bedroom. We were planning to be away for three-and-a-half years, staying until Pete had taken his GCSEs at the school in Kathmandu. There wasn't the option of doing A-levels in Nepal, and we thought it unfair to expect him to go to India for his schooling and cope alone with a whole new world; so it was known from the start that we'd be back in England in the summer of 1995.

We left early in 1992. In those days, the most economical way of getting to Nepal was to fly with a Bangladeshi airline to Dacca, stay overnight there, then fly to Kathmandu the next morning. The part of the journey that most stands out in my mind is the overnight stay in Bangladesh. Dacca is a busy, noisy Asian city, teeming with vehicles and people. At the gate of the hotel where we stayed there was an armed guard. Philip and Pete wanted to go for a walk after being cooped up for hours on the plane, but they returned quickly to the safety of the hotel. Women, begging, had been holding out their babies to them, and other beggars had wanted to take Pete's watch. Pete had never seen such poverty before. Philip commented later that if we had turned round and gone back to England right then, it would, even so, have broadened Pete's horizons for the rest of his life.

Having one's horizons broadened, however, can be a painful experience. And we were only just beginning. We duly went on to Kathmandu the next day, stayed at the INF guesthouse for a night, and then continued on by bus, over the steep, twisting roads, to Pokhara, which was to be our new home.

Pokhara is a beautiful town. To the north is a backdrop of snow-covered Himalayan Mountains. To the south is a large lake, Phewa Tal, lined on one bank with hotels, restaurants and shops geared towards tourists. In those days the INF community in the town was based on a mission compound where there were offices, a primary school for the children of missionaries, a language school for those of us new to the country, and accommodation for new people and others passing through. At first, we were to be lodged in a couple of rooms there, to have our meals in the communal dining room, and to get down as soon as possible to learning the Nepali language, customs and culture. For the first few months, Pete was to stay in Pokhara with us, and Philip and I were to be his teachers. Later, he would live in Kathmandu during term time and study at Kathmandu International Study Centre (KISC) to prepare for his GCSEs.

Philip and I had both lived in developing countries before, so it wasn't long before we began to feel at home. For Pete, however, it was all strange and new, and he desperately missed his friends back in Fleckney. But people were very kind. One Australian family took us for a lovely outing to the lake. We hired boats and rowed across to a little cove on the other side where the children swam, and we all chatted and ate our picnic. Another time, one of the missionaries offered Philip the loan of his motorbike so that he could take Pete on a trip to see another lake up in the hills where there was a fish farm. There was one other older boy in the INF community, an American lad of about fourteen who was being homeschooled by his parents. He and Pete became friends, and a kind young man, who had asked us how he could help Pete, bravely agreed to take the two lads white-water rafting. There was a tourist bus that left Pokhara early in the morning and delivered them back late in the evening – a long day, but a fantastic adventure.

Pete's schooling didn't go terribly well. I was responsible for the French classes and got quite frustrated when Pete deliberately mispronounced the French words! But his Nepali language was coming on well. It's easier to pick up a language when you're young than when you're in your fifties! And Pete, struggling to settle into formal classroom-learning, was instead playing a game a bit like shove-halfpenny with the young Nepali language helpers, so his conversational ability was coming on a lot better than ours!

In fact, even after three years there, we never spoke Nepali well. Our work was to be in English and it seemed inappropriate to spend the necessary hours of study and practice required to become fluent in Nepali. Perhaps it would have been self-indulgent, and pandering to my pride as a former student of Linguistics, to give the time to be really good at the language. We could say enough to get around, to go shopping and to communicate with our domestic helper at home.

Eventually we did have our own home. The mission rented the downstairs of a house in the town for us and we settled in, got ourselves equipped and made ourselves comfortable. The landlady, who lived upstairs with her family, asked if we could employ her sister to help us, and we were very happy to do this. Like many English people, I don't find it easy employing someone to work for me in the home, but in a country where there is a lot of poverty, you are actually doing them a favour – giving them the means of earning a little money. And from my point of view, as a housewife in a place without washing machines and vacuum cleaners, it was a huge help leaving the cleaning and laundry to someone else. So Ratna came to work for us each day. She had not lived in a town before and was quite scared of foreigners like us. One day she broke a cup and went upstairs to her sister in tears, expecting me to be angry. Her sister sent her down to tell me what had happened and to say sorry. Of course, I told her that it wasn't important; it upset me that she had even imagined I'd make a big thing of it, but we were still getting used to one another. Another time I asked her to go to the town and buy some groceries for me. She was away for ages and, when she got back, told me that she had been sitting at the roadside and enjoying watching all the people and vehicles going by. It had not dawned on me before that for someone who until then had lived in a remote village in the hills, going shopping in Pokhara was even more demanding than it would be for me to go to Oxford Street in London for a day.

Most of the work of the INF is medical. Because Nepal has more than one major religion, there was a law forbidding attempts to encourage people to change their faith. Most of the country is Hindu. Everywhere you go there are little temples with statues of the Hindu gods and devout worshippers bringing their offerings. But in the groups of the north and in the Tibetan refugee camps most people are Buddhists, and there are many monks in their saffron robes, strings of prayer flags fluttering in the breeze and the sound of prayer wheels whirring. In other parts of the country there are many followers of Islam, too. The law was an attempt to allow each community to follow their own faith without any animosity or attempts at proselytising. Until the 1950s, foreign missions were not given visas to work in Nepal, but in 1951 permission was given for a Catholic mission to start a boys' boarding school in Kathmandu, and the following year visas were granted for a team of four medical staff to start a hospital in Pokhara. This team had been working for thirteen years on the Nepal border in India, waiting and praying for the door to open to that country. Their medical skills were needed but of course they had to work within the law and were only allowed to speak about their Christian faith if someone asked them questions. That was the beginning of INF. With the two doctors went a Nepali couple who had been converted to Christianity in India. As nationals of the country, they could speak about their faith more freely than the foreigners, and without the danger of having their visas withdrawn.

By the time we were there, in the 1990s, INF had a contract with the government, renewable every five years, stating how many INF members they could bring into the country and specifying the qualifications they needed to have and the work they would do: doctors, surgeons, a dentist, specialists in tuberculosis, aids and leprosy, anaesthetists, nurses, physiotherapists, managers of medical programmes and so on. By that time, the handful of Nepali Christians from the 1950s had grown to thousands of believers in different parts of the country. In Pokhara there were already seven small churches. Don't imagine big Gothic buildings. These were just groups of believing people meeting in a room in someone's house or in a small building made for the purpose. The buildings were largely unadorned, with mats on the floor for people to sit on. As expatriate Christians, we were welcome to be part of these churches, but not in any leadership role. It was our duty to support, encourage and pray for our Nepali fellow believers, while doing our day-to-day work in a way that recommended the God we were serving. In Nepal, years of hard work and service could be cancelled out if the missionary lost their temper. To Nepalis, that was an awful weakness – not always easy for westerners to avoid. It is quite a challenge there, as in the West, to live in such a way that people ask how you come to be so peaceful, or so happy, or so kind. None of us could claim to have arrived, but we journeyed on.

Within that framework, Philip and I had been granted visas as a pastoral couple to care for the spiritual needs of the INF team. We felt responsible for everyone's wellbeing, just as when Philip was minister of a church at home. But of course, in a mission setting there were differences too. On one occasion, one of the INF members had to go to his home country for a brief visit because his father had died. His wife and children couldn't go with him because of the expense of travel, so Philip suggested that on the day of the funeral we would spend some time with them, so that they could all talk about their memories of their grandfather and thank God for him – and ask God to look after their grandmother now that she would be missing him. So we held a mini memorial service with them and they seemed to find it helpful. Another time we were asked to arbitrate when one of the INF team felt that he had been unfairly criticised about his work. We were able to get him together with the person who had hurt him and they were able to talk to each other, apologise and pray for one another. Most of our work, though, was with people who had deep-seated problems from the past to discuss, not connected to their daily work, which had surfaced because of the stress of adjustment to a new country and a different way of life. In some cases we didn't feel that we had helped as effectively as we would like to have done. In others we could only sit back in delight as we watched God working and saw people changed.

One was a mother of three young children whose husband was a doctor. From the first time we talked with her we could see that she was seriously depressed but as she trusted us more she spoke more freely, and shared that she sometimes felt suicidal and had walked to the edge of the gorge more than once, thinking of throwing herself over into the river below. Something in her childhood had left her feeling unloved and let down by her mother. For a while we couldn't put our finger on what it was, but then she fell and broke a bone – and remembered! Years before, when she was a child, she had broken her wrist, and at the hospital her mother had been told to wait outside the room while the bone was set. She had promised her daughter that she would be waiting just outside the door, but when the little girl came out, she couldn't see her mother, and had felt betrayed. Remembering now, she realised as we talked that, more than likely, some nurse had come along and insisted that her mother sit somewhere else while she was waiting. They wouldn't have wanted her in the doorway. We prayed for healing of that memory, that a new adult understanding would erase the childhood hurt. Shortly afterwards, when she was sitting on the veranda of their house one day, she saw an eagle soaring higher and higher and felt as if God was saying to her, "I will lift you up to a higher plane." But there was another related hurt. Her husband's work brought him into daily contact with a female colleague with whom he had a good friendship, and his wife was beginning to feel unloved and let down whenever she saw him chatting to his colleague. We asked to see her husband and talked and prayed with him. The years of his wife's depression had been hard on him too. However, a short time before we talked, he had been watching a film and something in the story had moved him to pray that God would help him to make his wife his best friend. We never needed to say anything to him about his wife's fears concerning his co-worker. God had already answered her prayer and the situation was changing. When our friend was not well, it had looked as if the family would have to return to their home country, and all her husband's expertise in tropical medicine would be wasted. Recently, however, Philip met them at a mission conference. She was radiantly well, and since that time they have put in many more years of medical work in a variety of countries. It is a delight to remember that lovely woman, and the fact that God did indeed lift her to a higher plane.

A lot of our work was less dramatic – just caring for the lonely and giving some feeling of family to those on their own. My years in Brazil had given me an awareness of the needs of the single ones, and we often invited folks for a meal or arranged little outings. On one of my birthdays, Philip and I on one motorbike and two of the single women on another went early in the morning to a vantage point where we could get a brilliant view of the sunrise over the hills. And after watching the view for a while we went to the lakeside and had a celebration breakfast at one of the restaurants there. Another time we met up with a couple of colleagues at a café by the lake to chat over their future. As we were going back home in the warm, dark evening, we passed crowds of tourists and Philip said to me, "Just think, all these people have spent thousands to have a holiday here – and we live here!" It was a wonderful assignment that God had given us.

Pete was away in Kathmandu by now, not finding it easy to be at boarding school, but beginning to adjust and enjoy being part of a multinational community. His best friend was a boy from the Seychelles. There was no opportunity to play football, because there weren't enough pupils in the school to make up the teams and no football field to play on, but they had great fun with basketball, and Pete got some tennis coaching for a while from one of the Gurkha officers at a camp not far from the boarding home where he was living. After the first few months at KISC, there were exams and end-of-term reports, and Pete came home to show us his with some embarrassment. In England he'd been able to coast along and get near the top of the class with minimal effort on his part. Now he'd overheard one of his friends say to another, "Oh look, I've got a B! I do like to get all As or A*s."

Pete realised that, as he put it, "Only the dummies in the class were worse than I was."

We pointed out that he had two choices. He could either carry on getting low grades, or he could pull out the stops and work a whole lot harder. We were very thankful that he made the decision to work harder, and adjusted to a better work ethic than is the norm for many teenage boys in England.

One huge advantage to his being at school in Nepal was the school trips. One year they went way up into the Himalayas to visit the Langtang Glacier. Pete was thrilled with some of the photos he was able to take. He had the bright idea of putting his snow goggles in front of the camera lens and produced some glorious pictures without any glare from the brilliance of the snow and ice. At the foot of the glacier is a lake of melting ice and the young people were able to swim in it, gasping at the cold but revelling in the sunlight and the uniqueness of the scene.

Another part of our work was travelling to visit some of the missionaries working in remote areas of the country. To get to some of the outposts, there was the possibility of going by a small plane. To others, we were able to use a bus or a mission vehicle. But to most places there was no road, just paths up and down the huge hills, and little houses by the side of the trail where we could buy cups of tea during the day or bed down in our sleeping bags at night. We had planned to visit one of those places just after Pete's half-term break. I'd had a tummy bug, so Philip had gone by himself to Kathmandu to spend time with Pete for his holiday weekend. When Philip got back, I seemed quite a bit better, so we set off on the three-day journey on foot, spent a few days there talking with the team, sharing their joys and problems, and left for the journey back to Pokhara. On the way back, we had to climb Omurai Hill, a steep, steep hill that seems to go on forever. I was struggling, only managing to take a few steps before I stopped for a breather, beginning to think I would never get to the top. One of our colleagues was with us and he kept telling me that near the top of the hill was a teahouse that sold cold Cokes – it sounded like heaven! When we finally arrived there, we found that it was quite a plush teahouse. They not only had cold drinks, but cold showers as well. The rest of the journey back must have been uneventful because I remember nothing more until we got home. I took my temperature and the tummy bug was back with a vengeance. My temperature was nearly 40°C.

Rural scene in Nepal

CHAPTER TWENTY-ONE

Coping with ME

1994 - 1995

Over the months since that tummy bug something seemed to be very wrong with me. Once, when we were chatting to a friend, I had to say, "Excuse me, I'm a bit tired today. Do you mind if I lie on the floor while we talk?" Too tired to sit in a chair? This was getting ridiculous! We realised that I was ill and there followed months of uncertainty. I had numerous tests both in Pokhara and at the United Mission to Nepal hospital in Kathmandu. The symptoms were varied but mostly subjective things that couldn't be measured – extreme lack of energy, painful limbs, erratic sleep patterns, over-the-top reactions to heat and cold – but the tests were all coming back negative. Some of my colleagues began to think it was psychological – was it just depression? I didn't think so. When I'd been depressed in Fleckney, a friend had asked me what I'd really like to do, and my answer had been, "Nothing except just curl up in bed and sleep." It wasn't like that now. I'd wake feeling good, thinking about what I'd do that day, but by the time I'd had a shower and cleaned my teeth, I was as weary as if I'd run a marathon.

Eventually one test came back positive. A blood test in Kathmandu seemed to give evidence of Kala-azar. Medication was available. All I needed was an injection of sodium antimony gluconate into a vein once a day for a month. I took the ampoules back to Pokhara and every day a wonderful colleague would come by on her motorbike after a busy day in the hospital and sit patiently injecting the chemical very slowly to minimise the pain. I was so grateful to her. I'm not someone who has a fear of jabs, but these were not easy injections to have. Seconds after the fluid went into the back of my hand, the veins higher up my arm would feel as if they were going into spasm. I was so thankful that she had the expertise and the patience to make it as easy as she could for me. By the end of the month, I was spending most of the day in bed.

Then I went back to Kathmandu for a further test to see if the injections had produced the desired effect. The doctor had said that if I was no better, she would want me to go back to England for further treatment. I didn't feel better, and the next blood test showed the same problem as before. So Philip brought over a bag I'd left ready and he and Pete saw me off on the plane to England and the Hospital for Tropical Diseases in Liverpool. A friend told me later that there had been a few tears when my plane disappeared.

I managed to do one useful thing on that flight! The plane was full of disappointed tourists. They had come to the beautiful country of Nepal expecting to see blue skies and wonderful snow-clad mountain peaks, but their travel agent had omitted to tell them that in the monsoon months, the skies are grey, the clouds are low and the mountain tops are invisible. As the plane gained height that afternoon, I noticed that we had climbed above the murk of the monsoon and I pointed out the Himalayan peaks to the man sitting by me. He quickly got out his camera and I realised that everyone else on the plane was following suit! They had seen some snowy summits after all!

Hilary met me off the plane and took me to their house in Lytham St. Annes for tea before we went to the hospital. Mum had come out of the nursing home so that we could all have tea together. She didn't like to see me looking so poorly and she shed a few tears too. That's the worst of being ill. Everybody else suffers as well as the one who's sick. But Mum had been tremendously brave about her stroke and the way her speech and mobility had been left so impaired. Now I thanked her for her courage and asked her to pray that I'd learn to be as courageous as she had been. After our meal, Harold took Mum back to the nursing home, and Hilary took me to Liverpool to the Hospital for Tropical Diseases.

In the end I was there for only a few days because the medics could find no evidence of Kala-azar. The phlebotomist in Kathmandu had made a mistake and all those poisonous injections had been unnecessary! It shocked me later when a friend working in that hospital wrote to me and asked if I'd be suing the hospital. "Of course not," I wrote back. "You could not have been kinder or more caring. There was no neglect by anyone. A mistake was made, that's all. Thankfully nobody has ever sued me for the hundreds of mistakes that I've made in my life!" (That experience has given me a horror of that type of litigation. Even now, when solicitors' firms come on the phone touting for business, asking if I've had an accident in recent months, I respond quite crossly, and tell them that they are serving only to put everyone's insurance premiums up!)

In Liverpool, they diagnosed me with Myalgic Encephalomyelitis (ME), also known as "chronic fatigue" or even "yuppy flu". I was discharged from hospital, and Harold and Hilary graciously looked after me at their house for a number of weeks. Harold, like many doctors, was somewhat suspicious about whether ME was a real illness at all, because it isn't measurable. Was it just psychosomatic? Hilary was slaving away in her big sister role, running up and down the stairs with trays and kindness. I was so grateful for that. Another benefit of being there was that I could see something of Mum. That was a great blessing because she died soon afterwards and I had memories to treasure of those few weeks.

Jon and Tim each drove up from Fleckney to St. Anne's for a day to see me. That was such a joy – to talk face to face, to catch up on all their news, to see them as men. Jon was already a committed Christian, so I could ask him about church as well as his work, and about how he and Tim were coping at home. Tim wasn't doing church at that time, but when he came, we had plenty to talk about with work and friends, and especially his music and the adventures of his band as they tried to get recognition. They were busy in the East Midlands and beyond but, like all bands, were eager to be noticed by representatives of the record companies. Exciting days! We tried to write regularly to the boys while we were abroad, but it was before the days of Skype and emails and, like most young men, they managed to write to us only occasionally. There is nothing like a face-to-face chat and a hug to feel close to one another. I was thrilled that each of them had given up a precious Saturday to come and see me.

One week, to give Hilary a break, I went down to Bryan and Janet's house in Essex. I have a special memory of one sunny day there. Janet was out and Bryan was working in the garden cutting back some bushes over their stream with an electric saw that he had hired. He came in at one point quite worried because he had slipped and dropped the hired saw into the water. It was no longer working! I said that he shouldn't worry about it – I was sure that if he left it open in the sunshine and came in for a sandwich and a cuppa, everything would be dried out and back to normal when he went out again. That proved to be right. It was important for me to notice that my role in the family wasn't the same as it had been when we were young!

Eventually I went back to Nepal, not well, and knowing that I'd not be very useful for some time – I'd have to rest a lot and wait to see how things went. You can imagine how that feels. I had gone to Nepal to serve the missionary community there, but instead I was spending most of every day in bed. I'd get up in the morning and have a shower; but would then need to rest for a few hours. Ratna would be around working – doing the washing, cleaning, preparing vegetables for the evening meal. I'd get up in the late afternoon to cook the meal and would sometimes sit at the table to eat with Philip. Sometimes we'd put it on a tray and he'd sit on the bed to eat his meal while I had to rest again. How useless was that! I read a lot of the books that were available in English, but found that I hadn't the concentration to read a book where the plot was at all complicated. Books by Dick Francis were my favourite fiction in those weeks; in them, the hero tells the story in the first person in the order it happens – I could cope with books like that. I could not get my head around anything more complicated. I felt utterly useless.

There were some consolations, however. Once, when Pete had been home for a holiday from school, I said I was really sorry not to have been able to do anything or go anywhere with him during the time he'd been at home. "Don't worry about that," he said. "I've known where you were and been able to find you every time I've wanted to talk." That was a comfort.

And there were stories in the Bible that became some of my favourite passages. One was the story of the poor widow who was putting her gift of two small coins into the temple treasury while Jesus and his disciples were watching. Others were putting in massive offerings, but Jesus said that she had given more than anyone. "They have given a small proportion of their riches, but she has put in all that she had."[5] I thought it related to me, not with regards to finances, but to energy. As far as physical energy was concerned, I was pretty destitute, but maybe I could concentrate enough to pray each day for colleagues in the mission, for Nepal, for Asia… And maybe Jesus would be pleased by my minimal offering. I felt as if he was.

I read over and over again the story of Job. God allowed all sorts of difficulties to come into his life – illness, loss of wealth, the death of his children – much greater problems than I had. But Job refused to give up on God in spite of all his suffering, and God told Job's friends that Job had reacted rightly. I began to see that it is of value in God's eyes for us to live through difficulties without giving up on him, hanging on to confidence in him whatever negative things he allows to happen to us. Maybe it's not just our work for him that pleases God, he also appreciates a steadfast faith that isn't daunted when the going gets tough. That became one of my most frequent prayers: "Don't let me get miserable, Lord. Don't let me fail you by complaining or being sorry for myself. Keep me thankful and able to praise you." He did. One part of me was aware of those who didn't understand the illness and thought I was a malingerer. I knew that I was a disappointment to them. And I was a disappointment to myself, useless, a failure. But the other part of me began to feel at peace. God understood. He knew what he was doing in my life even if nobody else did.

The months ticked on. I was still achieving almost nothing and it was nearly time for Pete to complete his exams in Kathmandu and for us to return to England. What were we going to do? Where were we going to live? Our house in Leicestershire had been the property of the church in the village so we had no home to go back to. Philip had no job. Pete would need to start his A-level courses somewhere. And I was still not well. Not the most brilliant prospect!

---

[5] See Mark 12:43.

KISC students at the boarding hostel.

CHAPTER TWENTY-TWO

Life in Birmingham

1995 - 2004

But in the event, thank God, it all worked out brilliantly. The INF office in Birmingham contacted Philip and asked if he would be willing to work there as a liaison between the mission and churches, part of the time in the office and part of the time travelling – either to see churches who were interested in supporting INF or were sending a missionary to Nepal and wanted to hear more about the country, or to talk with potential missionaries who were considering Nepal as a possible place to use their skills for God. With Philip's background as a minister and his experience overseas, this seemed an ideal job for him. He wrote back eagerly to say that he would be very happy to come to Birmingham and accept the appointment. The man in charge of the INF office at that time was Peter Hitchin and he offered to contact the sixth form college in Kings Norton, where his own boys had studied, and ask them to save a place for Pete. They did this, and we took Pete for an interview and to have a look at the school soon after we came back to England in July 1995. We also looked for a house in Birmingham within reach of the INF office in Harborne and the college in Kings Norton. It had seemed impossible that we'd be able to buy a house, but wonderfully, miraculously, two modest legacies, a gift and an interest-free loan from an anonymous benefactor added up to what was needed. 1995 was at the end of a very serious housing slump in the

UK, and we were able to get a three-bedroomed semi in Selly Park for only £58,000. Once again, God's arithmetic had been spot on!

Our first few weeks back in England were spent in Fleckney. Jon and Tim had met us at the airport and taken us to stay at the lovely home of a couple from the church who had offered us hospitality for as long as we needed it. It was a really good few weeks for us, hearing all the news from Jon and Tim, being welcomed back by our friends at church, catching up with our relatives and the other churches who had prayed for us and given us financial support in the years we'd been away. It was summer time and we so enjoyed the lovely meals people gave us – as well as all the strawberries! Our local garage owner in Fleckney is a Christian and our friend, and he had been thoughtful enough to set aside a good second-hand car that someone had brought in for sale – just what we needed. We had some furniture stored at Jon and Tim's house and there was other furniture available from my mother's bungalow now that she had passed away. All the details were falling into place.

On removal day, Tim drove me over to Birmingham. The rest of the family and some strong, willing friends were coming later with cars and a hired van full of our stuff. Tim and I were to meet the vendor outside the house and get the keys. To the embarrassment of the man we were meeting, his solicitor had said that he must not give us the keys as not all the money was yet in the solicitor's possession. I prayed inwardly. We stood talking on the pavement for a few minutes wondering how the day was going to turn out, picturing the busy Birmingham road lined all day with our van and cars while we twiddled our thumbs and waited. Then there was another phone call from the solicitor. "Yes, the final bank transfer has been received." The keys were ours. Apart from that hiccup, and later the considerable struggle for the men getting our heavy piano up the steps in front of the house, the day went smoothly, and it didn't seem long before we were sitting together eating bought pizzas and having a final chat with those who had to return to Leicestershire. Our new life was beginning.

Living in a big city was going to be a new experience for us and we were not particularly looking forward to it. I had not realised that once you know people in the area, your part of the city begins to feel like a village. And this part of Birmingham was well established and had plenty of wildlife in the gardens. During the years we were there, we had tadpoles in the little pond each spring, a hedgehog once in the border, a nest of baby squirrels in the tree just over our fence, visiting urban foxes when the weather was cold, lots of birds coming to feed and, most notably, a family of long-tailed tits coming to drink and bathe in the birdbath. And, of course, cities do have their compensations: a cosmopolitan community, great bus services, and occasional visits to musical events or to the theatre. Our Birmingham years were full of interest.

At first my health remained very poor. One afternoon, when Pete came in from college, I asked how his day had been. He replied and then said with a grin, "Have you had a busy day, Mum?"

"Oh yes!" I replied. "I got rather stiff lying on the settee, and had to get up and move the cushions to the other end!"

We both laughed. But gradually I was able to do a bit more, to walk to the church down the road, to take a bus to the supermarket, or to make a meal for visitors as well as ourselves.

Philip and I had felt it right to settle in a church just down the road – we needed a church within walking distance because Philip's job would take him away from home many weekends and I would have no car. At first Pete came with us but, now sixteen, he needed a livelier church with more young people. He found one that seemed to suit him for a time, but the pressure of trying to fit in at college became too much and he soon abandoned churchgoing altogether. After three years out of the UK, he had a lot of catching up to do to become one of the lads! Some of the staff at the college knew that he had just come back from living overseas, but he never mentioned it to his mates. Having missionary parents does nothing for one's street cred! Did coming from a Christian family mean that he had missed out on all the fun? Once he was invited to a late-night party in someone's flat with the promise of great music and lots of other young people. Somewhat reluctantly, we said that he could go if he wanted to, but asked him to make sure that he had money for a taxi home and that he didn't do anything that he'd be really ashamed of afterwards. We were in bed when he got back in the early hours, but I heard the front door as he let himself in. To my surprise, he put his head round our bedroom door, saw I was awake and whispered that he needed to talk. We crept downstairs so as not to wake Philip, and Pete gave me the story of the evening.

The party had been gatecrashed by a group of youths who had eventually walked off with all the expensive hi-fi equipment. The police had been called. And Pete had given his name as a witness. Quite a scary introduction to the "fun" of teenage life in Birmingham! When, eventually, the police had identified those responsible and the case came up, I went with Pete to the law courts and we sat waiting for hours, whiling away the time by chatting to the other witnesses. Pete was amused that I listened patiently to one young lad's detailed description of how to grow cannabis in a wardrobe with an electric light to give the plants warmth and light! The case wasn't heard that day because one of the defendants had not turned up; and the next time, Pete felt confident enough to go by himself. The only thing he wasn't sure about was going to the shops near college – apparently, the offending youths hung about near there and would now be able to recognise him. I felt for the other witnesses who actually lived in that area, and understood how hard it must be for people in that situation to be willing to come forward as witnesses.

There was a problem in the college with racism, mostly involving tensions between the boys of Afro-Caribbean origin and those from Asian families. Pete played basketball with some of the Afro-Caribbeans and became good friends with them but, to my horror, he began to come out with some unpleasant comments about Asians. After our years living in Asia, I couldn't believe what I was hearing. "Oh Pete, don't get drawn in to that sort of rubbish."

He must have had another think about it. A few days later he told me that, sitting in the college canteen, one of his friends had been writing a racist comment on the table and was shocked when Pete said to him, "Pack it in!" The boy didn't complete what he was writing, and Pete was glad.

The path from childhood to manhood is a rocky road. With all our boys we felt the pain of seeing them struggle to discover who they really are. Philip and I had decided together that our role was not to try to mould them to suit us, but to keep on loving and praying and to believe that eventually they would become whatever God had planned. Philip is better at it than I am. There's still a bit of the schoolteacher in me that, even now, can make me too free with my advice!

In those early years in Birmingham, Philip was happily occupied in his work with the INF, part of the time in the office and part of the time visiting many different kinds of churches to talk about Nepal. My link with Nepal was now minimal – occasionally I could host returning missionaries and once a month I had a day at the office stuffing envelopes with the regular mailings to mission supporters. I was glad that there was still something I could do.

Jon and Tim came over to Birmingham to see us from time to time. Once, when Philip was away, Tim came over for a couple of days' break, and one day drove Pete and me to Kidderminster where we caught a train on the Severn Valley Railway up to Bridgnorth. The boys were amused by my excitement at the nostalgic sights, sounds and smells of an old steam train – even the same scratchy upholstery that had prickled my legs on many a journey to the seaside when I was a child. I enjoyed that day so much that some years later we chose to celebrate our silver wedding anniversary by repeating that journey one Saturday with Bryan and Janet, Harold and Hilary and the boys and their girlfriends. It happened to be a 1940s day with sandbags around the station, a group of child evacuees on the train with their gasmasks and a spiv trying to sell black market nylons! When the train arrived at Bridgnorth, it was apparently in German hands and was renamed "Brucknord". We saw the spiv being arrested and taken away. And there was the sound of a gunshot. A chilling reminder for a moment of what could so easily have happened if there had been a different outcome to the Second World War. But the rest of the day was a delight, especially for the older members of the family. Bryan said he had never had a more nostalgic day.

Actually "the boys and their girlfriends" isn't quite the right description. Previously, there had been another memorable visit to Birmingham when Jon had come to see us with Tracey to tell us that they had become engaged. We were thrilled that he had chosen such a lovely girl and that they were planning their future together. By the time of our silver wedding expedition on the railway, Tracey was his wife. In the end, all the boys have married wonderful girls. We've joked that they have done a great job of choosing good daughters-in-law for us! I'm sure, though, that was not the first consideration in their minds when they made their choices!

But I'm getting ahead of myself. A true account of those years in Birmingham has to be bitter as well as sweet. The church Philip and I belonged to was going through a turbulent time and we had the sorrow of seeing many good friends leave and move on to other churches. What had been a very thriving church thirty years before when we were students at Bible college had now become quite small and weak. The minister moved on and for a time there were so few of us there that we could not afford to pay a minister's stipend and had to fend for ourselves. They were hard and discouraging years, but we still believed that God was alive and well and that he could give us a "hope and a future"[6]. We had many advantages: a good building at a bus stop on a main road, a united group of faith-filled people, several young couples who had come to the church as students and were now maturing and eager to work for God – and we had God himself. We didn't feel strong, but with almighty God...

Over the ensuing years, we saw something of what he can do. Our group of young graduates worked hard on refurbishing some unused Sunday school rooms, and we were able to lend one to an Anglican church just along the road who had a problem finding space for all the children at their church. We began a toddler group one morning a week and had the joy of making many friends of different races and different backgrounds. Once a month we held a fellowship lunch after the morning service where everyone brought food to be shared and we enjoyed eating together and deepening our friendship with one another.

An Alpha course was started. Those interested in finding out what it means to be a Christian met in the early evening for a meal, which was followed by us watching a video together and discussing what the video taught us.

One evening during the meal, one of the visitors was telling us how he managed to get quite a good income from claiming more than he was really entitled to from the benefits system, and then said casually to the man sitting next to him, "What job do you do?"

The man's reply came as a shock: "I work for the DHSS."

Sadly, our visitor didn't come back again. We were sorry, but understood why!

There were encouragements along the way. One day I was down at the church on my own – I think I was sorting a shelf of books that were there for people to borrow – when I heard someone coming into the building. She was a lady from Zimbabwe who had been passing on a

[6] Jeremiah 29:11 (NIV).

bus and had felt that God was telling her to get off the bus and come into the church. She told me her story. Her husband had been killed in the troubles in Africa, and she and her son had come to live in England where she had relatives. Recently, her son had died too. I told her that we had lost a son as well, and we hugged one another and prayed for one another – one of those lovely happenings that can only be planned by God. Another time, as I was walking down to church, one of our Asian neighbours asked me if anyone at our church would be willing to take on a cleaning job at the Pakistani embassy in the city. When I asked him why he wanted someone from church, he said that there is quite a lot of money around at the embassy and that those who work there need to be trustworthy. I felt so thankful that this man, though of a very different faith from ours, still felt that he could trust Christians. As it turned out, one of our friends was appointed for the cleaning job and, in due course, was asked to take on other responsibilities there as well.

We had encouragements, but we had our failures too. A personal failure of mine, which I still remember with shame, was when I was about to lead the service one Sunday morning. We were just about to begin, when one of our lovely Jamaican ladies came up to me in distress. As she had got off the bus, she had seen a man lying in the bus shelter, apparently drunk or asleep, but perhaps ill. Hilda was asking me what we could do to help him. But my mind was on what we were doing in church and I said, "If he's still there at the end of the service, we'll go across and help him." I could see that Hilda was not happy with that, but I just got on with starting the service and didn't give the man another thought until the service was over. By then, he was gone. Talk about "passing by on the other side" – that was me that day, too religious to stop and care. Not at all how Jesus would have been. But in spite of our failings, over the ensuing years we saw something of what God can do. Eventually the church was on an even keel financially and we were able to appoint another minister, a man of peace who has served there faithfully ever since. God was raising up new life from the ashes.

In our family too, God was at work. One Sunday evening Tim rang us with some great news. He had been giving an elderly great-aunt a lift back to Leicester from a family gathering at Jon and Tracey's in Nottingham, and in the course of the conversation she had asked Tim,

"What's going on between you and God these days?" I don't know what Tim had said in reply, but he had got home, prayed a heartfelt prayer telling God that he wanted to make a fresh start with him, and was now telling us. A whole new phase of his life was starting. Tears all round, but tears of joy this time.

The next time we saw Tim, he said to Philip, "Thanks, Dad, that you weren't on my back all the time. I knew what you must be thinking – you didn't need to say it." We were so glad that God had helped us not to nag, but just to love him and pray while God and Tim were sorting out which direction his life would go.

Not long afterwards, Pete was invited by Phil (a friend in Fleckney) to go down to London one Sunday to visit a church that Phil had been very much helped by. So Pete went to stay at Tim's house, go to church with him on the Sunday morning and go off to London with Phil on the Sunday afternoon. During the village service on the Sunday morning a song was announced, the words came up on the screen and everyone stood up to sing. Pete stood with them. Then, realising that there was not a single line in the song that he could honestly sing, he sat down again and found himself in tears. Tim and other friends gathered round him to pray. Later that day at the church in London, he made a new commitment of his life to the Lord. When Pete got home to Birmingham very late that evening, Philip and I were washing up after having a houseful of visitors that day. Pete stood in the kitchen doorway. "I've something to tell you that's a bit embarrassing," he said, "because it's like saying that you've been right all along and I've been wrong... I've come back to God and given my life to him." The washing up was forgotten for a while as we all hugged one another and thanked God for his amazing kindness to us as parents. All our boys were now committed to following Jesus. We'd not been perfect parents, we knew. We'd made many mistakes, but God had overruled all that and won each of our lads for his kingdom.

Chapter Twenty-Three

Where Are We Now?

2004 - 2017

Now let's fast-forward more than a dozen years to today. Jon and Tracey have given us two lovely, bright granddaughters, Nathania and Isobel, now aged fourteen and twelve. Tim has found a wonderful wife in Claire, and they have a happy, sporty young son, Dillon, who is ten. Pete is married to our dear Annika and they have two lively-minded children, Chloe, who is ten, and Isaac, who is seven. We delight in being grandparents and watching each personality develop in its own way. What potential!

For a few years after retirement from the INF office, Philip returned to the pastorate, leading a small church at Stourport-on-Severn in Worcestershire. When he finally retired at seventy years of age, we bought hiking boots and imagined ourselves going for long walks in that beautiful countryside. We have great memories of one such walk on a winter's day in the Wyre Forest, when the snow was pristine and glorious and the only other footprints on the path were those of rabbits and birds. But latterly, the boots didn't often make an appearance! It's partly because we were slowing down and didn't have the energy we once had. But it was also partly because we had got busy again with other things: continuing to serve our church in various ways, helping to care for some of our elderly and lonely friends, running a small door-to-door business selling eco-friendly goods, working with an outreach to young people in the town, trying to grow fruit and vegetables on our allotment, and so on. When we felt it was all getting a bit much, we reminded ourselves that we'd rather be busy than bored, and thanked God that we could still be useful.

My brother Bryan died nearly four years ago. He was just eighty. The success of his professional life was celebrated by an obituary in the Guardian. The success of his home life is demonstrated by his three able children, his grandchildren and even two little great-grandsons. In June 2013, Bryan rang to tell me that an inoperable cancer had been discovered, and he had learned that he was likely to die within two months.

"Oh, Bry..." I said, "is your faith helping at all?"

He replied through tears, "There's a verse from the Bible that I can't get out of my mind: 'Underneath are the everlasting arms.'"

Once during those two months, in a conversation with Hilary, he said, "I've always known that there is a God, and I've always known that he is kind."

That reminded me of when he was first a student at Cambridge. On the first Saturday afternoon there, he had found himself alone, with nothing planned and nowhere to go. Loneliness hit him like a staggering blow. Talking about it afterwards he said that he had prayed asking God to send him someone to talk to.

"Did God send someone?" I remember asking.

"No, but somehow it didn't matter then."

I didn't understand then, but see now with more mature eyes that even an unanswered prayer may have been part of the discovery that God is kind, the sort of person you can talk to and know that you have been understood. Bryan was an intellectual and had often struggled with some aspects of faith, but it was a great comfort for us to know that, in spite of his questioning, there was a rock-like basis of faith to see him through those difficult weeks and beyond.

Hilary has been a widow for several years. For thirteen Christmases since Harold's death, she has been each year to help at Crisis in London. She books in at a Premier Inn for a few nights and spends her days at a Crisis centre, caring for those of the guests who come for a haircut. She makes sure that the volunteer hairdressers have adequate supplies of all that they need, and she welcomes the guests, showing them where to sit and wait their turn, smiling and chatting, just being a source of acceptance and love to homeless, lonely people. She is now eighty-two, but she plans to carry on helping at Crisis as long as she can. Last year she went to Nepal for a couple of weeks. A medical referral centre had been built in Nepalganj with money she had given in memory of Harold, and she had the privilege of being part of the opening ceremony there.

There are still moments when I am the little girl, somewhat in awe of my big brother and sister. But very proud of them!

Philip and I have been married for forty-one years now and have moved away from Worcestershire to be near to one of the boys – Jon who lives in Nottingham with his family. We thought that in view of our advancing years it made a lot of sense to move near to one of the family in case we need help one day. Being old is something I struggle to get my head around. I know it as a fact and see the evidence of it when I look in the mirror, but when I see this old lady with her wrinkled skin, glasses and hearing aid, it seems laughable – as if the real me is masquerading in someone else's body. The real me inside feels about nineteen, just on the verge of being an adult, just beginning to feel a bit more confident and able to cope with life! Do we all feel like that, I wonder?

One amazing answer to prayer has been a change in my eating habits! All my adult life I have been somewhat overweight – I've mentioned it once or twice in my story here – eating quite reasonably for much of the time, but when I was overtired or feeling a bit down, my eating would become out of control and I would eat compulsively, especially if there was some chocolate around. This felt a huge failure for someone who was trying to bring her whole life under God's control, and frequently I'd tell God how sorry I was. Until next time. But a couple of years ago, I had the awful experience of seeing something of the reality of how God feels as he watches me invading the biscuit tin yet again, his pity and compassion for the helplessness of a failing human being, his grief that a person he has helped so much still has so far to go... That experience has done more to change me than all the years of useless resolutions, and I thank him for the measure of success in the months since. How incredibly patient he is with us all!

In coming to Nottingham we really have retired and for a few months have had hardly any responsibilities except trying to get our new home sorted and to find room to stow all the things we've acquired over the years. But we are hoping that our coming here won't mean signing off from being involved in God's plans to bless and help humanity. So we are looking around and asking God to show us some little ways that we can be useful to him and can serve his kingdom.

Now, looking back over the ups and downs of my life, one little human life, short and insignificant in terms of the whole of human history, I thank God that he took this child with all her faults and areas of weakness and somehow fitted her into his great cosmic jigsaw puzzle. As the children's song says:

Our God is a great big God.
Our God is a great big God.
Our God is a great big God
And he holds us in his hands.

He's higher than a skyscraper.
He's deeper than a submarine.
He's wider than the universe
And beyond my wildest dreams,
And he's known me and he's loved me
Since before the world began.
How wonderful to be a part
Of God's amazing plan![7]

True for me. And true for all of us. How exciting is that!

---

[7] *Great Big God,* Hemming, Nigel / Hemming, Jo,

Family weekend to celebrate my 80th birthday

Contact the Author

To contact the author, please write to:

Joan Kearney
c/o Onwards and Upwards Publishers
3 Radfords Turf
Exeter
EX5 7DX

Or send an email to:

joan@kearney.me.uk

What Shall I Read Next?

It's Alright Now, God is in Charge

Patricia Margretta Cassidy

ISBN 978-1-907509-84-1

"There are no Europeans left on the Hill; we should have gone too! Everyone else was evacuated early this morning! We must all go immediately!" The words came tumbling out.

There was no time to argue; it was now known clearly that the Japanese Army had invaded Malaya and was rapidly making its way southwards. In the surrounding area everyone had fled. There was no traffic, no movement anywhere, just silence.

The Second World War and the events that followed shaped Patricia's life as her family travelled from country to country and across three continents. From tigers and bandits to submarines and war camps, the stories of her family highlight the risks, dangers and sufferings experienced in Asia and Africa during that important historical period. Yet we also see how faith in Jesus can guide a family through every trial.

Riding High With Jesus

Colleen Hurd

ISBN 978-1-911086-32-1

From early childhood years in rural South Africa to retirement years ministering in UK rest homes, Colleen Hurd's testimony shows how God often leads us on unexpected paths in order for us to reach our divine destiny.

Colleen's journey takes her around the world, including an extended period in Israel. As she simply makes herself available to serve wherever she is, miracles and remarkable events unfold.

Colleen shares her joys – such as her growing family, new ventures, God's provision and encouragement, and supernatural encounters – as well as her sorrows – such as her husband's sudden death, difficult relationships and financial loss. Yet she demonstrates how God uses all things to lead her forwards, unfold His purposes, and bring compassion and comfort to the lives of those around her.

This is a faith-inspiring story that you will not want to miss!

Available from **www.onwardsandupwards.org** and all good bookshops.